T

SYRACUSE

FAN'S

SURVIVAL GUIDE TO THE ACC

THE SYRACUSE FAN'S SURVIVAL GUIDE TO THE ACC

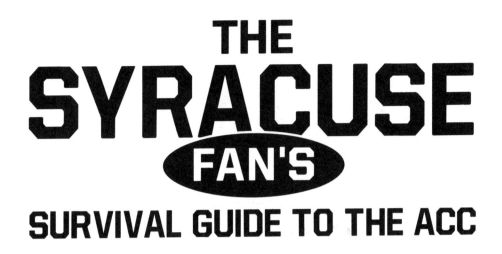

MIKE WATERS · MARK BIALCZAK

REEDY PRESS
St. Louis, Missouri

Reedy Press
PO Box 5131
St. Louis, MO 63139, USA
www.reedypress.com

Library of Congress Control Number: 2013939561

ISBN: 978-1-935806-49-3

Design by Jill Halpin

Printed in the United States of America
13 14 15 16 17   5 4 3 2 1

CONTENTS

PREFACE

Goodbye Broadway! Hello Tobacco Road!

Syracuse University's departure from the Big East Conference and subsequent move to the Atlantic Coast Conference in the fall of 2013 will bring about many significant changes for the Orange athletic programs, its coaches, its players, and its fans.

The Big East is the only conference that Syracuse and its fans have ever known. In the days prior to the Big East's formation in 1979, Syracuse participated in the Eastern College Athletic Conference (ECAC), but that loosely knit organization did not operate as a conference and did not include football.

Syracuse rose to national power along with the Big East. In fact, the two are so intertwined that it's hard to determine whether the Big East lifted Syracuse's profile or if Syracuse helped the Big East's rise to prominence. Syracuse played in the Carrier Dome, its feud with Georgetown gave the Big East a rivalry game, and Pearl Washington became one of the Big East's first stars for a league built on big markets and big personalities.

But Syracuse leaves the Big East behind and ventures into a new world of college athletics. Gone are traditional rivalries with Georgetown and St. John's. In their place will be games against North Carolina and Duke. The annual trip to New York City for the Big East Tournament will be replaced by sojourns to Tobacco Road and the ACC Tournament, the granddaddy of all conference tournaments.

Syracuse fans have gained a well-earned reputation for traveling to cheer on the Orange. Syracuse graduates and transplanted Central New Yorkers turn out in droves to see Syracuse play on the road. Syracuse's road map, however, has changed. No more familiar trips to Philadelphia, Providence, and Piscataway. Instead, Syracuse fans will travel to Charlottesville, Chapel Hill, and Clemson. Syracuse fans will need a new information source as they follow the Orange into the ACC and here it is: *The Syracuse Fan's Survival Guide to the ACC.*

There will be some familiar stops on the way to the ACC. Former Big East brethren Boston College, Miami, and Virginia Tech made the jump to the ACC back in 2004 and 2005. Pittsburgh and Notre Dame are moving into the

ACC along with Syracuse. And in the next year, Louisville will also leave the Big East in favor of the ACC.

Syracuse has few ties with the ACC's remaining members. Syracuse played Georgia Tech in the 2004 Champs Bowl, but that game didn't turn out so good for the Orange. And in 1987, Syracuse met North Carolina in the East Region finals at the Meadowlands. That one went a little better as Syracuse advanced to the Final Four. But Syracuse has never played at Duke's Cameron Indoor Stadium, and Syracuse has never played at Clemson's Death Valley.

This guide is designed to help ease the transition to the ACC for Syracuse fans. There are tips on finding the right place to stay in Miami, where to eat in Chapel Hill, or where to go after a game in Atlanta. There's a list of important phone numbers, details on tailgating, and ticket information. There's more background on each school's history, the football and basketball programs and their traditions.

Since Syracuse will be hosting ACC fans for the first time on a regular basis, there is a section on Syracuse as well. ACC fans can also utilize this book on their trips to Syracuse as well as a resource to find new places to stay and eat in the familiar ACC locales.

The 2013 football season will mark Syracuse's entry into the ACC. The ACC has placed Syracuse in the Atlantic Division along with Boston College, Clemson, Florida State, Maryland, North Carolina State, and Wake Forest. In 2013, Syracuse plays home football games against Boston College, Clemson, Wake Forest, and Pittsburgh. Syracuse's ACC road trips will be to Florida State, North Carolina State, Georgia Tech, and Maryland. The trip to Maryland will be a first-and-final for Syracuse since Maryland will leave the ACC for the Big Ten after the 2013-14 year.

Yes, the college sports landscape is changing. This resource guide should make the Syracuse fan's drive down Tobacco Road a little easier and a lot more enjoyable.

—Mike Waters and Mark Bialczak
February 2013

ABOUT THE ACC

The Atlantic Coast Conference actually did begin on Tobacco Road. And one of the first names suggested for the league was the Tobacco Conference.

On May 8, 1953, the seventeen member schools of the Southern Conference held their annual meeting at the Sedgefield Inn near Greensboro, North Carolina. During this session, seven schools decided to withdraw from the Southern Conference. Those seven schools—Clemson, Duke, Maryland, North Carolina, North Carolina State, South Carolina, and Wake Forest— would become the charter members of the ACC.

But it took a while before the new conference settled on a name. Several newspapers in the region received suggestions from fans. Some of the potential names included Dixie, Mid-South, Mid-Atlantic, Seaboard, Colonial, Blue-Gray, Piedmont, Southern Seven, and, yes, even Tobacco. One suggestion just barely missed the mark: Shoreline.

Duke athletic director Eddie Cameron came up with the idea of calling the new league the Atlantic Coast Conference. On June 14, 1953, the seven schools' representatives met again; this time in Raleigh, North Carolina, where the league's bylaws were adopted and its name officially became the Atlantic Coast Conference. Each of the seven schools contributed two hundred dollars to pay for the new conference's expenses. The monetary sums would change a bit over the years to today's astronomical athletic department budgets and television contracts.

On December 4, 1953, the seven ACC schools met again; this time back at the Sedgefield Inn in Greensboro. One of the results of this meeting was to admit the University of Virginia as the ACC's eighth member. The ACC's membership would remain the same for the next eighteen years. Wake Forest athletic director James Weaver was installed as the ACC's first commissioner on May 7, 1954. He remained in that position until his death in 1970. The ACC's Student-Athlete of the Year Award was named for him.

The ACC's membership remained fairly stable for its first fifty years. Until the recent shifts in the college landscape, the only withdrawal of a school from the ACC happened in 1971 when South Carolina left the conference. South Carolina officials had chafed at the heavy influence that four North Carolina schools held over conference matters, including sites for the conference tournament and admission standards for athletes.

The ACC's membership stayed at seven until 1978 when Georgia Tech joined the conference. Georgia Tech had been a charter member of the Southern Conference, but broke away along with several other schools to form the Southeastern Conference in 1932. Tech withdrew from the SEC in 1964 because football coach Bobby Dodd thought the SEC's rule limiting the number of scholarships was resulting in some schools running players off in order to sign more recruits. Years later, the NCAA would enact rules limiting the number of scholarships for each school, leveling the playing field nationally. Georgia Tech, which had found life as an independent difficult, became a member of the Metro Conference. In 1978, Georgia Tech joined the ACC for all sports.

The ACC remained an eight-member conference until 1991 when a wave of expansion began to change the sports map. Miami joined the Big East Conference and it looked like Florida State might join Miami, but at the last minute FSU officials accepted an offer from the ACC, which saw the Big East's addition of both Sunshine State schools as a threat to its Southern borders.

The ACC's membership steadied for another ten years, but then in the spring of 2003 the conference made a bold move. The ACC invited Syracuse, Miami, and Boston College to leave the Big East and join the ACC. But the governor of Virginia, realizing that a depleted Big East would damage Virginia Tech's athletic department, blocked the move. Now, a deal had to include Virginia Tech. Syracuse officials worked to stabilize the Big East. The ACC extended invitations to Miami and Virginia Tech, and both schools accepted. Meanwhile, Syracuse and Boston College remained in the Big East with the league's membership pledging their allegiance to the conference.

A few months later, however, Boston College officials bolted from the Big East; a decision that would bring lawsuits from several Big East schools. Miami and Virginia Tech would join the ACC in 2004, while Boston College had to remain in the Big East until 2005.

In September 2011, Pittsburgh and Syracuse announced that they were leaving the Big East for the ACC. The two former Big East schools will become full-time members beginning with the 2013 football season.

In 2012, the University of Maryland decided to leave the ACC for the Big Ten. Maryland's departure marked the first withdrawal of a school from the ACC since South Carolina in 1971. Officials in the ACC responded to the loss of Maryland by adding Louisville as a full-time member and Notre Dame for all sports except football. Notre Dame announced in March that it would join the ACC for the 2013-14 season. Louisville is expected to begin play in the ACC in the fall of 2014.

While many conferences have been looking to broaden their geographical scope, the additions of Syracuse, Notre Dame, and Pittsburgh—and in a year's time Louisville—will serve to strengthen the ACC's footing while keeping the conference entirely within the eastern time zone. Syracuse will help bridge the gap between Boston College and the Virginia schools.

Syracuse, Pittsburgh, and Louisville have succeeded in many sports besides football and basketball. Notre Dame, while not a full member in terms of football, will play five football games a year against ACC schools. Those games against the Fighting Irish will mean more national television coverage for ACC teams.

The additions of Syracuse and Pittsburgh allowed the ACC to reopen contract talks with ESPN. In May 2012, ESPN and the ACC announced the terms of an amended contract that extended their current twelve-year deal another three years through the 2026-27 season. ESPN will pay approximately $3.6 billion to the ACC over the course of the deal. That deal figures to pay each of the ACC's schools roughly $17 million a year. That amount represented a $4 million increase of the ACC's previous contract with the network.

Pittsburgh and Syracuse might have made the decision to leave the Big East based for football reasons and the financial incentives that sport offers, but the two Northeast schools will be joining a league with a rich tradition in all sports. Six different schools from the Atlantic Coast Conference have combined to win a total of fifteen NCAA titles in men's soccer, including Wake Forest in 2007, Maryland in 2008, Virginia in 2009, and North Carolina in 2011. The ACC has won twelve men's lacrosse championships with the most recent being Virginia in 2011 and Duke in 2010. Six different ACC teams have appeared in the College World Series since 2006. Maryland has won six field hockey championships. Wake Forest has won the NCAA men's golf title three times. North Carolina's women's soccer team has won an astounding twenty-one NCAA titles.

But while there is athletic excellence on all fields and the football money drove Syracuse and Pittsburgh to leave the Big East, the Atlantic Coast Conference is at its heart a basketball league.

Everett Case is regarded as the father of ACC basketball. The former

North Carolina State coach brought an exciting brand of basketball to the region. He pushed for the construction of Reynolds Coliseum, which was the largest college basketball arena in the country when it opened in 1949 with a capacity of 12,400. Reynolds Coliseum became the site for many ACC and NCAA tournaments plus the Dixie Classic, which annually featured the four North Carolina schools.

The ACC Tournament became the league's highlight event. While most conferences sent their regular-season champion to the NCAA Tournament, in 1961 the ACC changed its bylaws to designate the tournament champion as the conference's representative. The importance of winning the conference tournament focused attention on the ACC. The ACC would continue this tradition until the NCAA began granting bids to more than one school from the same conference following the 1975 season.

In leaving the Big East, Syracuse and Pittsburgh will see the end of many longtime natural rivalries. Syracuse's most noted rival has long been Georgetown, but only in basketball. Syracuse also has a shared history with Connecticut, St. John's, and Villanova. Pittsburgh's closest rival, West Virginia, left the Big East for the Big 12 after the 2011-12 season. The Panthers' rivalry with Villanova is for basketball only and Penn State competes in the Big Ten.

When Syracuse, Notre Dame, and Pittsburgh join the ACC, the two schools will be reunited with their former Big East brethren—Boston College, Miami, and Virginia Tech. In 2014, Louisville will come on board, giving the ACC a very Big East-like feel. But Syracuse, Notre Dame, and Pittsburgh fans will notice many differences in the ACC. While many schools in the Big East share arenas with NBA and NHL teams that are spacious and sterile, the ACC plays in on-campus gyms that are cozy and often hostile. Duke's Cameron Indoor Stadium is one of the most notorious places to play in the country, but Clemson's Littlejohn Arena is tough on opposing teams, too. You want tradition? North Carolina has so many jerseys hanging from the rafters of the Dean Smith Center that the school had to impose criteria in order to limit the number—National Player of the Year or two-time All-American.

Basketball may be king, but the ACC plays some football, too. Clemson's stadium isn't known as Death Valley because of the heat. Virginia Tech is a national program. The man whose name is on the most famous trophy in sports, John Heisman, coached at Clemson and Georgia Tech. And there's nothing like the sight of Chief Osceola planting his spear at the fifty-yard line.

Michael Jordan played in the ACC. So did David Thompson. Ralph

Sampson. Tim Duncan. Grant Hill. Dean Smith coached in the ACC, as did Lefty Driesell, Norm Sloan, Bones McKinney, and Jim Valvano. Mike Krzyzewski, the only college coach with more career victories than Syracuse's Jim Boeheim, still stalks the sideline in front of the Duke bench.

The ACC is the Four Corners, Howard's Rock, the Cameron Crazies, and the tomahawk chop. Oh, it's going to be a heck of a ride, Syracuse fans. Welcome to Tobacco Road.

Boston College

Boston College was founded in 1863 with three teachers and twenty-two students. The Jesuit school was located in Boston's South End, and its curriculum focused on theology, philosophy, Greek, Latin, and English. Shortly after the turn of the century, the college had outgrown its urban setting and moved to Chestnut Hill. The Recitation Building, now known as Gasson Hall, opened in 1913. Gasson Hall remains an iconic feature on the BC campus to this day.

Boston College fielded its first football team in 1893. In 1914, Boston College played two home games in Fenway Park. The original Alumni Stadium opened the following season, but BC would continue to play games at Fenway through the 1950s.

In 1940, Frank Leahy, a twenty-nine-year-old Knute Rockne protégé, became the head coach at Boston College. In his first year, Leahy guided the Eagles to a 9-1 record. BC, ranked eleventh, was invited to the Cotton Bowl, becoming the first team from New England to play in a bowl in twenty years. Trailing 6-3 late in the game, the Eagles drove to Clemson's eight yard line but couldn't score. The following year,

BOSTON COLLEGE

STUDENTS
14,500

CHESTNUT HILL
pop. 11,078

ALUMNI STADIUM
44,500

SILVIO O. CONTE FORUM
8,606

COLORS
Maroon & Gold

NICKNAME
Eagles

MASCOT
Baldwin

CAMPUS ATTRACTIONS
Chestnut Hill Reservoir,
Gasson Hall,
Devlin Hall/McMullen
Art Museum

PHONE
617-552-8000
(general information)

617-552-4444
(campus police)

617-552-3000
(athletic department)

TICKETS
617-552-3000 or
www.bceagles.com/tickets

Leahy's Eagles went 10-0 and rose to No. 5 in the rankings. The Eagles faced No. 4 Tennessee in the Sugar Bowl. This time, BC won, scoring the game's last twelve points for a 19-13 victory.

After Boston College lost to Alabama in the 1943 Orange Bowl, the Eagles went almost forty years before playing in another bowl game. In 1982, Doug Flutie, then a sophomore, restored BC's gridiron glory, leading the Eagles to the Tangerine Bowl. It was the first of three straight bowl appearances for BC in the Flutie era. Flutie topped off his illustrious career with a Heisman Trophy and a win over Houston in the 1985 Cotton Bowl.

Since then, Boston College has produced a number of outstanding players, many of whom have gone on to the NFL. Names like Bill Romanowski, Mark Chmura, Matt Hasselbeck, Damien Woody, Chris Hovan, and Matt Ryan have sustained Boston College's success.

While football at Boston College dates back to the 1800s, the Eagles' first basketball game was on December 26, 1904. Boston College made its first NCAA Tournament appearance in 1958. In 1963, Bob Cousy, the former Boston Celtics great, took over as BC's head coach. In six seasons, Cousy led the Eagles to a 117-38 record. In 1965, the Eagles received their first NIT bid. In 1966, BC posted its first win in either the NCAA or NIT with a 96-90 win over Louisville in the first round of the NIT. The Eagles went 23-3 in 1966-67, including wins over Connecticut and St. John's in the NCAA Tournament. In Cousy's last season, Boston College went 24-4, advancing to the finals of the NIT before losing to Temple.

Chuck Daly, the Hall of Fame coach who would later win NBA titles with the Detroit Pistons, took over after Cousy left. Daly remained at BC for just two years.

The program survived a point-shaving scandal involving members of the 1978-79 team. The scheme involved gamblers and members of the mafia, including Henry Hill, whose story was later the basis for the movie *Goodfellas*.

Boston College joined the Big East in 1980. The basketball program continued to be a haven for outstanding coaches, including Dr. Tom Davis, Gary Williams, and Jim O'Brien. Players such as Michael Adams, Jay Murphy, Dana Barros, Bill Curley, Danya Abrams, and Troy Bell have continued BC's proud tradition. In 2003, Boston College left the Big East for the ACC. The move angered many principals at other Big East schools, as the members of the Big East had pledged their loyalty to the league following the departures of Virginia Tech and Miami. Boston College was cast as the Big East's villain for the next two years until the Eagles began play in the ACC in 2005.

Football

NATIONAL CHAMPIONSHIPS (0): Boston College's 1940 squad finished with an 11-0 record and a No. 5 ranking, the highest ranking in school history. The Eagles went 10-0 in the regular season and then beat undefeated Tennessee, 19-13, in the Sugar Bowl.

ACC CHAMPIONSHIPS (0): BC played and lost the 2007 and 2008 ACC Championship games.

BOWL RECORD: 13-9 (.590). Last bowl—20-13 loss to Nevada in 2011 Fight Hunger Bowl

LONGEST WINNING STREAK: 16 games (twice), 1927-29

WINNINGEST COACH: Tom O'Brien (1997-2006), 75-45, 62.5 percent

HEISMAN TROPHY WINNERS OR HIGHEST HEISMAN FINISH (1): Quarterback Doug Flutie, 1984 winner

Basketball

NATIONAL CHAMPIONSHIPS (0): BC has never appeared in the Final Four. The Eagles have made the region finals three times—1967, 1982, and 1994.

ACC CHAMPIONSHIPS (0): BC has never won the ACC Tournament. The Eagles' best regular-season finish in the ACC was third (11-5 record) in 2005-06.

NCAA TOURNAMENT RECORD: 22-19 in eighteen appearances. Most recent appearance: The 2009 team lost to Southern California, 72-55, in the first round.

WINNINGEST COACH: Al Skinner (1997-2010), 247-165 (.599)

NATIONAL PLAYERS OF THE YEAR: Troy Bell was a second-team All-American in both 2001 and 2003.

LEGENDS

Doug Flutie

Doug Flutie became a starter in the fourth game of his freshman year at BC. He led the Eagles to a 30-11-1 record and three bowl games as a starter. As a senior in 1984, Flutie completed 233 passes for a school-record 3,454 yards. The Eagles went 9-2, including a 45-28 victory over Houston in the Cotton Bowl. But the game that stands out to this day is BC's 47-45 win over Miami in which Flutie heaved the last-second pass to Gerard Phelan for the game-winning touchdown as time ran out. Flutie received the Heisman Trophy in 1984.

Mike Ruth

Ruth is the best interior lineman—offensive or defensive—to ever play for Boston College. In his career from 1982 to 1985, Ruth recorded nearly 300 tackles and two dozen sacks. In 1984, he had 102 tackles, 76 of them solo. He won the Outland Trophy as the nation's best interior lineman despite the fact that Boston College had a losing record that year. It's the only time that a player off a team with a losing record has won the Outland Trophy.

Dana Barros

Dana Barros was the Big East Rookie of the Year in 1986 and followed that up with three straight years on the All-Big East team. He was the first BC player to score 2,000 points in his career, and his total of 2,342 points remains third on the school's all-time list. He later played thirteen seasons in the NBA.

Bill Curley

Bill Curley scored 2,102 points and grabbed 996 rebounds in his career at Boston College from 1991 to 1994. Both figures rank fourth in school history. Curley helped lift the BC hoops program out of a three-year run of losing records. In his last three years, Curley's teams went to the NIT twice and then the NCAA in 1994. As a senior, Curley led the Eagles to within a game of the NCAA Final Four.

ARENA

Silvio O. Conte Center: The successful campaign to build a new football stadium motivated BC alumni to back the construction of a gymnasium to house both the basketball and hockey teams. In 1958, the Roberts Center, a 4,400-seat arena, opened on the BC campus.

In the mid-1980s, the success of the program and BC's membership in the Big East Conference necessitated a larger on-campus arena. The Conte Forum, named for former U.S. congressman and BC alumnus Silvio O. Conte, opened in October 1988. Conte Forum is also home to the school's hockey team. The arena seats 8,606 for basketball and 7,884 when configured for hockey.

Conte Forum is adjacent to Alumni Stadium. Some luxury boxes overlook both the football field and the basketball court/hockey rink.

STADIUM

Alumni Stadium: Boston College plays its football games in Alumni Stadium, which dates back to 1915. The original Alumni Stadium was located in the middle of the BC campus on the site of where the Campus Green is today. In the 1930s and 1940s, the Eagles outgrew Alumni Stadium and began playing home games at Fenway Park and Braves Field, which housed Boston's two major league baseball teams. In the 1950s, BC president Joseph Maxwell started a campaign to build a new on-campus stadium. On September 26, 1957, the new Alumni Stadium opened as BC hosted Navy. A capacity crowd of more than 26,000 attended the game. The game between BC and Navy was put together by then-U.S. Senator John F. Kennedy. Navy ruined the opening of BC's new home with a 46-6 win over the Eagles.

CUSE CONNECTION

ALL-TIME FOOTBALL RECORD VS. SYRACUSE: 18-28

Last meeting November 27, 2010: Boston College 16, Syracuse 7

ALL-TIME BASKETBALL RECORD VS. SYRACUSE: 23-40

Last meeting February 16, 2005: Boston College 65, Syracuse 60

Pearl's shot: The shot that sparked a legend happened on January 16, 1984, in a game between Syracuse and Boston College. In the final seconds of the game, Syracuse led No. 16 Boston College, 73-71, but the Eagles' Martin Clark got the rebound off a missed free throw, made the basket, and got fouled. With four seconds remaining, Martin went to the line with a chance to win the game. Martin missed, and Syracuse's Sean Kerins snared the rebound. He threw the ball to freshman guard Dwayne "Pearl" Washington, who took a few dribbles and launched a shot from half court. The ball ripped through the net. The Carrier Dome crowd went into a frenzy. As the Syracuse players and coaches celebrated, Washington streaked down the sideline and ran straight down the tunnel to the team's locker room. A legend was born.

The Diamond Ferri game: On November 27, 2004, Syracuse traveled to Chestnut Hill to face the seventeenth-ranked Eagles. Syracuse (5-5) was coming off an embarrassing loss to Temple. Boston College (8-2) needed a win to clinch the Big East's BCS bowl bid. Adding to the drama was the fact that this was BC's last year in the Big East before leaving for the ACC, and the bitterness between the two schools was palpable. Syracuse's star running back Walter Reyes was hurt and would not play. His backup, Damien Rhodes, got hurt early in the game. That forced SU coach Paul Pasqualoni to turn to defensive safety Diamond Ferri. The Boston-area native had played tailback in his first two years at SU. Ferri played both offense and defense, rushing for 141 yards and two touchdowns while also intercepting a pass and returning it for a touchdown. He also returned two punts. Ferri's iron-man performance helped Syracuse to a 43-17 upset of the Eagles.

MASCOT

The Eagle became Boston College's mascot in 1920 after Father Edward McLaughlin took offense at a cartoon in a Boston newspaper that depicted BC's championship track team licking clean a plate of its rivals. McLaughlin wrote a letter to BC's student newspaper, pointing out the need for a mascot. "And why not the eagle, symbolic of majesty, power and freedom?" wrote McLaughlin. "Its natural habitat is the high places. Surely, the Heights is made to order for such a selection."

OTHER SPORTS

Most of Boston College's athletic successes have come on water, either open water or the frozen kind. The Boston College men's hockey team has won five NCAA championships. The first came in 1949, but the last four came in 2001, 2008, 2010, and 2011. In addition, BC can claim six national championships in sailing, although the NCAA does not recognize the sport. The women's sailing team won the Intercollegiate Sailing Association's championship in 2008 and 2012, while the coed team has won four titles.

"For Boston"

Boston College is known as the birthplace of the college fight song. T.J. Hurley, BC Class of 1885, wrote the lyrics to "For Boston." Since then, the song has served as the standard for many college fight songs.

For Boston, for Boston,

We sing our proud refrain!

For Boston, for Boston,

'Tis Wisdom's earthly fane.

For here all are one

And their hearts are true,

And the towers on the Heights

Reach to Heav'ns own blue.

For Boston, for Boston,

Till the echoes ring again!

For Boston, for Boston,

Thy glory is our own!

For Boston, for Boston,

'Tis here that Truth is known.

And ever with the Right

Shall thy heirs be found,

Till time shall be no more

And thy work is crown'd.

For Boston, for Boston,

For Thee and Thine alone.

GAME DAY

MEDIA

Broadcasting the Game: WEEI-AM 850 in Boston, WEEI-FM 103.7 in Providence, WBZ-AM 1050 in Boston

Covering the Eagles: www.bostonglobe.com/sports (*Boston Globe*), www.bostonherald.com/sports (*Boston Herald*)

TAILGATING

Tailgating at football games is a huge challenge at the Boston College campus. The area around Shea Field is the main tailgate area. It's adjacent to Alumni Stadium. However, you must have a parking pass, and those passes go to BC donors. If you have a game ticket, you are allowed to walk onto Shea Field and visit with tailgating parties. So if you're a Syracuse fan, but you have a friend who is a BC donor and hospitable in nature, you're in luck. There are some areas around campus where fans can park and set up picnics.

For families, there is the Fan Fest in the Flynn Recreation Complex. The Fan Fest includes inflatables and face painting for kids.

SHUTTLE

The city of Boston has a robust public transportation system known as the T. Many fans headed to BC games park elsewhere in the city and ride the T to the BC campus. In addition, there are satellite parking lots in Brighton and Needham where fans can park for free and then ride a shuttle that drops off right in front of Alumni Stadium.

TRADITIONS

Superfans: Each year, the freshmen at Boston College get a gold Superfan T-shirt. Each year has a new design so each class is distinctive. The students keep that T-shirt for their entire college career, and they wear the gold shirts at BC football and basketball games. The tradition started in 1997 when two students—Jeff Bridge and Chris Millette—wanted to boost the student atmosphere at BC's athletic events.

The Bronze Eagle: At the start of the 2006 football season, a bronzed eagle statue was unveiled right outside the BC locker room. The BC players all touched it before going onto the field. The Eagles upset No. 18 Clemson, 34-33, in double overtime. The very next week, BC knocked off No. 23 BYU, 30-23, also in double overtime. Two thrilling wins over nationally ranked teams in two weeks turned the eagle statue into an instant tradition.

ABOUT TOWN

The village of Chestnut Hill is located six miles west of Boston. Chestnut Hill does not refer to a single hill; instead, the name reflects a series of small hills that overlook the Chestnut Hill Reservoir. Chestnut Hill itself sits just two hundred feet above sea level. The village is not incorporated; none of the villages in Massachusetts are incorporated. In fact, Chestnut Hill is actually part of three different counties. It's Brighton and West Roxbury neighborhoods are technically part of the city of Boston and Suffolk County.

Chestnut Hill is best known as the home of Boston College. The area around the campus and the reservoir was developed by world-famous landscape architect Frederick Law Olmsted, who also designed New York's Central Park.

LODGING

The Marriott Newton: The Boston Marriott Newton hotel is located right along the Charles River. Guests can dine in the hotel's restaurant overlooking the Charles. Rates here will be better than the hotels in downtown Boston, and this hotel is just five miles from the BC campus. *2345 Commonwealth Ave., Newton, MA 02466, 617-969-1000 or 800-228-9290, www.marriott.com/hotels/travel/BOSNT-Boston-Marriott-Newton*

The Bertram Inn: The Bertram Inn was built in 1907 by a wealthy tobacco owner, who then gave the Inn to his daughter as a wedding present. The Inn is located in Brookline, just outside Boston and close to the BC campus. There are sixteen guest rooms, some with working fireplaces. The Bertram also has a sister inn—the Samuel Sewall Inn. *92 Sewall Ave., Brookline, MA 02446, 617-566-2234 or 800-295-3822, www.bertraminn.com*

The Boston Park Plaza: Hotels in downtown Boston can be outrageously expensive, but the Boston Park Plaza offers elegance and the opportunity to get a decent room rate. It's located in the center of everything; just two hundred yards from Boston Common. *50 Park Plaza at Arlington St., Boston, MA 02116, 800-225-2008, www.bostonparkplaza.com*

EATING

The Eagle's Deli: Located in Cleveland Circle, just a Doug Flutie heave from the BC campus, the Eagle's Deli offers everything from a full breakfast menu to sandwiches (try the reuben) to milk shakes. It's all topped by the twelve-pound Eagle burger, which was featured in the Travel Channel show *Man vs. Food*. *1918 Beacon St., Brighton, MA 02135, 617-731-3232, www.eaglesdeli.com*

Cantina Italiana: One of Boston's richest traditions. Cantina Italiana is the oldest restaurant in Boston's famous North End. The restaurant, which opened in 1931, features a wide variety of Italian dishes. (Our personal fave? The Saltimbocca di Pollo.) *346 Hanover St., Boston, MA 02115, 617-723-4577, www.catalinaitaliana.com*

Mike's Pastry: No matter which restaurant you go to, you must top off your evening in the North End with a visit to Mike's Pastry's for a cannoli. *300 Hanover St., Boston, MA 02113, 617-742-3050, www.mikespastry.com*

Fleming's Steakhouse: Situated on the edge of Boston's historic theater district, Fleming's stands out as the place for steaks, chops, and seafood. This is a high-end joint, which offers car service from points throughout Boston as well as private dining rooms for groups of eight to one hundred. *217 Stuart St., Boston, MA 02116, 617-292-0808, www.flemingssteakhouse.com/locations/ma/boston*

SIGHTSEEING

The Freedom Trail: Boston is unique among the nation's larger cities in that it enjoys a well-deserved reputation as a walking city. Hence, the Freedom Trail is the best way to see the city's most noted sites. The Freedom Trail includes Boston Common, the Granary Burying Ground, the Old North Church, and the Boston Massacre site. There are guided and self-guided tours available at the Boston Common Visitors Center located at 148 Tremont Street. *Boston City Hall, One City Hall Square, Boston, MA 02201, 617-635-4500, www.cityofboston.gov/freedomtrail*

Fenway Park: A tour of legendary Fenway Park is a special event for sports fans, even if you're not a Red Sox fan. The guided tours last one hour and take visitors all around the park from the Green Monster in left field to the Pesky Pole in right. Tickets for a tour of the stadium are available on the day of purchase only and on a first-come, first-serve basis. *4 Yawkey Way, Boston, MA 02215, 617-226-6666, boston.redsox.mlb.com/bos/ballpark/tour.jsp*

SHOPPING

Faneuil Hall Marketplace: Also known as Quincy Market, this vibrant shopping area is in the middle of downtown Boston. It's next to historic Faneuil Hall and the Freedom Trail cuts right through it. Visitors can find everything here from small merchants to large retailers plus dozens of dining options. *www.faneuilhallmarketplace.com*

Newbury Street: Welcome to Boston's version of Rodeo Drive. Newbury Street consists of eight blocks of salons, boutiques, and restaurants. The area used to be part of Boston Harbor until it was slowly filled in during the 1800s and became the city's Back Bay section. This is no urban shopping mall. Newbury Street oozes individuality and style. *www.newbury-st.com*

NIGHTLIFE

Lansdowne Street: Why go to one bar or nightclub when you can pick from dozens? Right next to Fenway Park is Lansdowne Street, which boasts the highest concentration of bars and entertainment venues in Beantown. There's the Cask 'n Flagon, an iconic baseball bar; there's the Bleacher Bar, which overlooks Fenway; or The Lansdowne, the ultimate Irish bar.

Coolidge Corner Clubhouse: The Coolidge Corner Clubhouse, or the CCC, opened in 1993. It started with five TVs, but now boasts twenty LCD televisions and every sports channel imaginable. Make no mistake, this is a Boston bar. The patrons love the Red Sox, Celtics, Bruins, and Patriots. They also love the Eagles as the bar is just two miles from the BC campus. *307 Harvard St., Brookline, MA 02446, 617-566-4948, www. thecoolidgecornerclubhouse.com*

LAST-MINUTE TIPS

Where to Shop: The Mall at Chestnut Hill offers a number of shops and restaurants close to Boston College. *199 Boylston St., Chestnut Hill, MA 02467, 617-965-3038*

Where to Buy Tickets: There are a number of ticket brokers in Boston, but a reliable one is Boston-based Higs Tickets, which has ticket pickup at both the TD Garden and Fenway Park. *1-877-SOX-TIXX, www.higstickets.com*

Jerry Remy's Sports Bar and Grill: Jerry Remy was a pretty fair ballplayer and a very popular announcer for the Boston Red Sox, but now he's the owner of a spectacular sports bar. The place is huge and so are the two 6.5 × 11-foot "screen monsters." In addition, there are thirty high-def TVs (sixty inches each) around the bar. The food is great and the beer selection is extensive. There's a rooftop deck that overlooks Fenway Park's right-field wall. *1265 Boylston St., Boston, MA 02215, 617-236-REMY, www.jerryremys.com*

And if you're not near Fenway, try Jerry Remy's Seaport, which features the thirty-two-foot HD video wall. It's the biggest and best sports wall aside from the Green Monster itself. *250 Northern Ave., Boston, MA 02210, 617-856-7369, www.jerryremysseaport.com*

TRAVELING TO CHESTNUT HILL?

The Boston College campus is located just outside of Boston in Newton. Boston's Logan Airport is eleven miles from the campus, but driving time fluctuates greatly depending on traffic. Boston is an easy five-hour drive from Syracuse via the New York State Thruway and Massachusetts Turnpike (I-90).

Clemson

CLEMSON UNIVERSITY

STUDENTS
19,914

CLEMSON
pop. 13,946

MEMORIAL STADIUM
81,750

LITTLEJOHN COLISEUM
10,000

COLORS
Orange, Purple, & White

NICKNAME
Tigers

MASCOT
The Tiger and the Tiger Cub

CAMPUS ATTRACTIONS
South Carolina
    Botanical Garden,
Walker Golf Course,
Fort Hill Plantation

PHONE
864-656-3311
(general information)

864-656-2222
(campus police)

864-656-1935
(athletic department)

TICKETS
800-CLEMSON or
www.clemsontigers.com

Philadelphia native Thomas Green Clemson traveled extensively throughout the United States and Europe, developing an appreciation for formal scientific education as well as agricultural affairs and farming.

A trip to the foothills of South Carolina led to an introduction to the daughter of famous statesman John C. Calhoun. They married in 1838. After the Civil War, Clemson remained despite the economic ruin, running his Fort Hill plantation to prosperity.

After his death, he earmarked the land and part of his financial estate for the establishment of an educational institution to teach scientific advances for agriculture. In November 1889, Governor John Peter Richardson accepted the gifts and began Clemson Agricultural College. Four years later, Clemson College opened its doors to 446 male military students. It remained a military school until 1955.

In 1964, it changed its name to Clemson University. Today, campus officials are proud of Clemson's designation by *U.S. News and World Report* as the nation's twenty-fifth best public university.

A tradition from the military school days remains today at the humongous football stadium known as Death Valley. Back in the day, freshmen had to hold their headwear, called ratcaps, aloft until the end of the homecoming game. Further, after every football loss, they had to hold the ratcaps waving in the crowd until the next victory. Today's students get away a little easier. At football games, all will wave their hands high, thumbs-folded under to signify the holding of a cap, until after the singing of the alma mater.

Famous sports alumni include football wide receiver Dwight Clark, forever etched in the minds of gridiron fans for hauling in from San Francisco 49ers quarterback Joe Montana the reception known thereafter simply as "The Catch," a touchdown grab that pushed the 49ers past the Dallas Cowboys and into the 1982 Super Bowl.

On the hardwood, Littlejohn Coliseum was the home for twin basketball players Harvey and Horace Grant. After two seasons, Harvey transferred to Oklahoma before going on to play in the NBA for a dozen years. Harvey Grant likely is the most popular former Clemson Tiger of Syracuse fans, too. His son, Jerami Grant, turned in a marvelous freshman season in 2013 for the Orange basketball team.

One of the seven charter members of the Atlantic Coast Conference, Clemson is known as a football school. Why not? In the football-crazy South, the Tigers have compiled an overall record of 668-450-45. And every home-game Saturday, fans travel from throughout the state to pack Memorial Stadium, and a town of 13,000 swells to more than 89,000. The Tigers have rewarded them by winning a national championship on the gridiron, beating iconic Nebraska 22-15 in the 1982 Orange Bowl under the guidance of Head Coach Danny Ford.

Yet Ford is not the most famous Clemson football coach. That honor goes to Frank Howard. In thirty years leading the Tigers, Howard won six ACC titles. The field at Memorial Stadium was named after Howard in 1974. And how's this for hard-nosed tradition? In the 1960s, a friend gave Howard a big rock for good luck. Howard's Rock now sits in a pedestal on the hill above the stadium. Players gather round to rub the rock to capture some of that good fortune before sprinting down to the field before every home game.

The current Tigers are led by Coach Dabo Swinney, who guided the Tigers to their fifth-best season ever, an 11-2 year that was capped by a last-second, 25-24 victory over LSU on New Year's Eve 2012 in the Chick-fil-A Bowl. The 2013 season holds much promise, with quarterback Tahj Boyd considered an early Heisman Trophy candidate.

Football

NATIONAL CHAMPIONSHIPS (1): 1981

ACC CHAMPIONSHIPS (14): 1956, 1958, 1959, 1965, 1966, 1967, 1978, 1981, 1982, 1986, 1987, 1988, 1991, 2011

BOWL RECORD: 17-18 (.486). Last bowl—25-24 over LSU in 2012 Chick-fil-A Bowl

LONGEST WINNING STREAK: 15 games, 1947-1949

WINNINGEST COACH: Frank Howard (1940-1969), 165-118-12 (.559)

HEISMAN TROPHY WINNERS OR HIGHEST HEISMAN FINISH: Although John Heisman, for which the trophy was named, coached at Clemson from 1900 to 1903, the Tigers have not had a winner. Steve Fuller and C.J. Spiller both finished sixth in the voting, in 1978 and 2009, respectively.

Basketball

NATIONAL CHAMPIONSHIPS (0): Clemson's best finish in the NCAA Tournament came in 1980, when shooting guard Billy Williams led the Tigers to a record of 23-9 on the way to the Elite Eight.

ACC CHAMPIONSHIPS (1): 1990

NCAA TOURNAMENT RECORD: 9-11 (.450) Last appearance—Lost 84-76 to West Virginia in the first round of the 2011 tournament.

WINNINGEST COACH: Cliff Ellis (1984-1994), 177-128 (.580)

NATIONAL PLAYERS OF THE YEAR (0):

ACC PLAYER OF THE YEAR (1): Horace Grant (1987)

The basketball Tigers, meanwhile, hover around the .500 mark all-time. The Tigers have qualified for the NCAA Tournament eleven times since 1980. Their best tourney showing was to the round of eight in 1980, when coach Bill Foster led them to a record of 23-9 while falling to UCLA 85-74 in the regional final.

Cliff Ellis was ACC Coach of the Year twice in his decade-long tenure, in 1987 and 1990, as his teams went 177-128 overall. The aforementioned Horace Grant was ACC Player of the Year in 1987.

The Tigers have been successful on the court since the days of Ellis's predecessor, Bill Foster, who guided them to a record of 156-106 from 1984 to 1994. Rick Barnes, currently the successful coach at Texas, had a good run at Clemson, going 74-46 from 1994 to 1998. Following a downturn under Larry Shyatt, whose teams were 70-84 from 1999 to 2003, Oliver Purnell led a resurgence to 138-88 from 2003 to 2010.

The current coach is Brad Brownell, Brownell's first squad went 22-12, followed by a 16-14 year in 2011-12, and hovered around .500 in 2012-13.

LEGENDS

John Heisman

This is the guy for which they named the granddaddy of all college football awards. Heisman was the athletics director at the New York Downtown Athletic Club when that award began in 1935. He coached at Clemson for three years, from 1900 to 1903. Heisman was known as an offensive innovator and champion of the forward pass. His greatest coaching success came at Georgia Tech, when he won the national championship in 1917. Lesser known is the fact that he also coached baseball at Clemson from 1899 to 1904.

Wayne "Tree" Rollins

Rollins was a 7-foot-1 center known as a defensive force for the Tigers. He was a third-team AP All-American for his senior season. Upon his graduation in 1977, he went on to play in the NBA for eighteen seasons. During his professional career, he became the fourth all-time leader in blocked shots. Rollins' No. 30 jersey is retired at Clemson.

Horace Grant

Grant was the twin that stuck around at Clemson, rewarding Tigers fans with stellar play after brother Harvey decided to transfer to Oklahoma. Horace Grant won the coveted ACC Player of the Year Award and was second-team AP All-American his senior year, 1987. He was drafted by the Chicago Bulls and won three NBA titles on the great Chicago teams with Michael Jordan, and another in 2001 with the Los Angeles Lakers. Grant retired as a Laker in 2004.

Dwight Clark

Clark played wide receiver for the Tigers before being drafted quietly in the tenth round by the San Francisco 49ers in 1979. And that was only because 49ers head coach Bill Walsh needed somebody on the Clemson campus to help him work out more noted Tigers senior, quarterback Steve Fuller. Clark snared "The Catch" in the back of the end zone in the NFC championship game, and went on to win two Super Bowls with San Francisco. The photo of his soaring No. 87 jersey is still a classic.

William "The Refrigerator" Perry

This defensive lineman was so big he blocked out all daylight. He earned his nickname when a teammate tried to squeeze past him into an elevator and proclaimed him to be as big as the biggest kitchen appliance. Perry was part of Clemson's national championship team and was a consensus first-team American as a junior in 1983. In the NFL, he joined the Chicago Bears. His nickname was shortened to "The Fridge" as he won a Super Bowl and got time on the offensive side of the ball to obliterate defenders near the goal line.

C.J. Spiller

Upstate New York football fans know Spiller best as a speedy running back and kick returner with the Buffalo Bills. At Clemson, Spiller was a consensus All-American, a former track star running like the wind past opponents. In fact, he set the NCAA record for kickoff returns for touchdowns with seven before being drafted No. 9 overall by the Bills in 2010.

NOTABLE ALUMS

Strom Thurmond
South Carolina governor and U.S. senator

C.D. Davies
CEO of Lending Tree and now QBE First

Harry Ashmore
Pulitzer Prize winner for public service in 1958

Nancy O'Dell
Former Miss South Carolina who went on to host *Access Hollywood* and has co-hosted the popular *Entertainment Tonight* syndicated show since 2011

Lee Brice
Notable country singer whose song "Woman Like You" went to No. 1 in 2012

STADIUM

Memorial Stadium: Since its construction in 1941-42, Memorial Stadium has picked up a nickname that strikes fear into the hearts of opponents. "Death Valley," packed with more than 80,000 loud and proud, orange-wearing Clemson fans, is an imposing sight and sound. Memorial started its life as a 25,000-seater. A series of expansion projects have made it the second-biggest stadium in the ACC. There are several stories that go along with the scary nickname. The field indeed lies low in a valley, and on a hill above sits the campus cemetery. And, in 1948, Presbyterian College coach Lonnie McMillian told sports writers he feared taking his team into Clemson's "death valley," where it never won and rarely scored. Lots of coaches have felt that dread since. The Tigers have won more than 70 percent of their games there, for a record of 227-88-7.

ARENA

Littlejohn Coliseum: Littlejohn Coliseum is named after James Corcoran Littlejohn, Clemson class of 1908, who was the college's first business manager. It opened in 1968 and holds 10,000 for basketball. It has been renovated twice, the latest of which added practice facilities so important to basketball recruiting. Both the men's and women's teams play tough at Littlejohn, which is considered cozy if you're a Clemson fan and intimidating if you're a visitor. Both Tigers basketball squads have home winning percentages of better than 70 percent.

ALL-TIME FOOTBALL RECORD VS. SYRACUSE: 0-1

1996 Gator Bowl: Syracuse 41, Clemson 0

ALL-TIME BASKETBALL RECORD VS. SYRACUSE: 2-0

1960: Clemson 78, Syracuse 67

2007: Clemson 74, Syracuse 70 (NIT, third round)

Thank you, Mr. Grant: Harvey Grant produces basketball players, pure and simple. The former Clemson, Oklahoma, and NBA star has seen three sons go on to play major college basketball. The eldest, Jerai, played at Clemson. The middle, Jerian, plays at Notre Dame. And, as cheered about often by Syracuse fans last season—including in a Carrier Dome game in which SU beat the Fighting Irish—youngest Jerami Grant was a tall, springy, and hot-shooting Orange freshman last season.

The color orange: Syracuse and Clemson will share their primary team color. Syracuse fans visiting the Clemson campus can feel pretty secure wearing their Orange shirt if they fold their arms across their chest to hide the school name. As far as orange-wearing teams go, Tennessee's is too pale and Texas's is too brown. Clemson's orange is just about the same as Syracuse's.

Mighty McNabb: The 1996 Orange rang in the New Year by blanking an astonished Clemson team. Freshman quarterback Donovan McNabb threw three touchdown passes, two to Marvin Harrison, and ran for another as unranked Syracuse walloped No. 23 Clemson. The Orange led 20-0 by the fourth quarter.

NIT tangle: Syracuse had beaten South Alabama and San Diego State in the Carrier Dome before falling 74-70 to the Tigers at Clemson in the third round of the NIT in 2007. K. C. Rivers of the Tigers dropped twenty-nine on the Orange, who were led by Eric Devendorf's twenty-three points. Clemson moved on to Madison Square Garden, where the Tigers beat Air Force before falling to West Virginia in the NIT title game.

Opening game clash: In the first game of the 1960 season, in the Midwest Invitational, the Tigers disposed of the Orange 78-67. Clemson lost the next game to host Kent State and went on for a season record of 10-16. Syracuse, coached by Marc Guley, went on to finish 4-19 that season.

MASCOT

It's said that 1896 football coach Walter Riggs brought along jerseys and the nickname from his previous school, Alabama Polytechnic Institute. You know it now as Auburn. They were the Tigers, and so, too, became the Clemson squad. The Clemson Tiger roams the sidelines in an orange costume, much like Syracuse's beloved and fuzzy Otto. The mascot must do pushups equaling the Tigers' score after every Clemson touchdown. In 1993, the Tiger was joined by the Tiger Cub.

OTHER SPORTS

Football isn't the only Clemson program with a national championship. The Tigers have won the big prize twice in men's soccer (1984 and 1987) and once in men's golf (2003). And, like most of the southern-most ACC schools, Clemson prides itself on its strong baseball and softball teams, as well as the men's and women's track squads. Like Syracuse, Clemson also fields competitive crew shells for men and women. But the Tigers, Syracuse fans should note, are not one of the ACC schools that field men's or women's lacrosse teams.

"Tiger Rag"

Long ago way down in the jungle

Someone got an inspiration for a tune

And that jingle came from the jungle

Became famous mighty soon

Thrills and chills it sends through you

Hot so hot it burns you too

Though it's just the growl of a tiger

It was written in a syncopated way

More and more they yell for the Tiger

Everywhere you go today they're shoutin'

Where's that Tiger?

Where's that Tiger?

Where's that Tiger?

Where's that Tiger?

Hold that Tiger!

Hold that Tiger!

Hold that Tiger!

C-L-E-M-S-O . . . N!

GAME DAY

MEDIA

Broadcasting the Game: WCCP 104.9 FM in Clemson

Covering the Tigers: www.upstatetoday.com (*Clemson Daily Messenger*); www.greenvilleonline.com (*Greenville News*); www.thestate.com (*The State*, Columbia); www.thetigernews.com (Clemson campus); espn.go.com/clemson-tigers (ESPN Clemson blog)

TAILGATING

Tailgating is allowed, and food and beverages are permitted. The only concern is large parties of twenty-five or more setting up beer kegs. About 25,000 cars need to be parked in the Clemson area on game day, and those big bashes can take up too much room. Visitors are directed to lots at the Campus Beach & Recreation area, about two miles from the stadium. Parking costs $20 per vehicle.

Parking for basketball is easier, with a lot available about four hundred yards from the coliseum. It's free, on a first-come, first-served basis. Information is available at www.clemson.edu/campus-life/campus-recreation.

SHUTTLE

Shuttle motor coaches are available at the university beach lots. They start about three hours before the game. They also run during the game in case fans need to get back to their car for any reason. They run until ninety minutes after the conclusion of the game. Information is available at www.clemson.edu/inside-clemson.

TRADITIONS

Running down the hill: Don't get to Memorial Stadium late, or you'll miss the site of one hundred-plus football players dashing down the grassy slope to the playing field. Oh, before that amped-up sprint, the Tigers all take part in another Clemson tradition, rubbing Howard's Rock for good luck.

Tiger push-ups: Picture, if you will, a football Saturday in which the Tigers hang (for them) a modest thirty-five points on the opponent. That would lead to the Tigers sideline mascot doing a grand total of 105 push-ups, all while dressed in a costume that weighs more than forty pounds (and that's before sweat issues). They would come in increments of seven, fourteen, twenty-one, twenty-eight, and thirty-five. And the Tigers have been known to score way more than thirty-five.

Tiger Paws: In 1970, Clemson decided to use a paw print as its logo. A real Bengal Tiger paw print was sent from the St. Louis Zoo for the model. Now, that tiger paw is seen on football helmets, campus sidewalks, and, yes, highways leading into town.

ABOUT TOWN

Clemson University used to be located in Calhoun, South Carolina. No, they didn't move the dorms or build new academic buildings. In 1943, the town changed its name to reflect the importance of the university to the area. Clemson is considered part of a tri-city area that also includes Greenville and Anderson. Yes, Clemson officially is designated as a city, even though residents

consider it a smallish college town with a population of about 14,000; Pickens County is home to about 110,000.

Clemson sits on the far west of South Carolina, in the foothills of the Blue Ridge Mountains and the shore of Lake Hartwell. Civic leaders take pride in the recreational activities, including extensive biking trails and a boardwalk at Lake Hartwell. For big-city action, Charlotte, North Carolina, is a two-hour drive northeast, and Atlanta is a two-hour drive southwest.

LODGING

James F. Martin Inn: The Martin is the campus hotel and conference center. It promises luxury in a scenic setting. Rooms overlook the lake, botanical garden, and golf course. One of the points of pride is what the Inn calls its "Pawsitively Purrfect luxury bedding." Prices are on the upper end. *240 Madren Center Dr., Clemson, SC 29634, 888-654-9020, www.clemson.edu/ centers-institutes*

Hampton Inn: Sports fans are listed first as those welcome to this edition of the mid-priced chain that serves free breakfast. It's just one mile from campus, off Highway 76/123. How's this for a sports-related address: *851 Tiger Blvd., Clemson, SC 29631, 864-853-7744, www.hamptoninn.hilton.com*

There's no shortage of chain hotels in the area with a wide range of rates, including Holiday Inn Express (864-654-8833); Marriott Courtyard (864-654-8833); Comfort Inn (864-653-3600); Sleep Inn (864-653-6000); and Days Inn (864-653-4411). In fact, a drive down Tiger Boulevard will pass most of these.

EATING

Pixie & Bills: Since opening in the summer of 1971, Pixie & Bills has gained the reputation as Clemson's original fine dining destination. The restaurant is open for lunch and dinner. The distinguished setting includes a fireplace, antique furniture, and fine art. Patrons can choose from steak, seafood, and specials. *1058 Tiger Blvd., Clemson, SC 29631, 864-654-1210, www.calhoun-corners.com/pixies*

Calhoun Corners: This is a fine dining restaurant with a rich history. The handmade brick building was constructed in 1893 and served as the community social center and then general store. It became a restaurant in 1974, until a fire destroyed it in 1997. Calhoun Corners was reconstructed using as much of the original material as possible. It sits next to the old Amtrak station, which now houses the Chamber of Commerce and Train Museum. *103 Clemson St., Clemson, SC 29631, 864-654-7490, www. tigergourmet.com/calhoun*

Brioso Fresh Pasta: With restaurants in Ashville, North Carolina, and Greenville, South Carolina, as well as Clemson, Brioso promises Italian countryside dining "sous vide" style. Its motto is "Pasta is our Passion. Fresh is our Obsession." *360 College Ave., Clemson, SC 29631, 864-653-3800, briosopasta.com*

SIGHTSEEING

Fort Hill Plantation: Visitors can imagine what it was like to live in the mansion with nineteenth-century statesman John C. Calhoun. The estate was originally owned by Calhoun's wife, Floride, and her mother. After a two-year restoration, Fort Hill Plantation reopened in 2003. It's listed as a national treasure in the Save Our Treasures program. Artifacts abound. *102 Fort Hill St., Clemson, SC 29634, 864-656-2475, www.clemson.edu/about/history*

South Carolina Botanical Gardens: Nature lovers will find a feast for their eyes at this 295-acre garden. The grounds includes streams, nature trails, a sculpture collection, and the Campbell Geology Museum. A stroll will reward visitors with the sight and smells of four hundred varieties of camellias, as well as hollies, hydrangeas, magnolias, and native plants. *150 Discovery Lane, Clemson, SC 29631, 864-656-3405, www.clemson.edu/public/scbg*

SHOPPING

The Tiger Sports Shop and The Athletic Department: I.M. Ibrahim, considered the father of Clemson soccer, founded these T-shirt emporiums in 1974. There's so much Clemson apparel they need two Clemson locations. The Tiger Sports Shop is at 364 College Ave. and The Athletic Department is at 1102 Tiger Blvd. They have the same phone number and web address: 800-933-7297 and www.tigersports.com.

If big box stores are your need, there's a big mall in Anderson, eleven miles away, and a smaller mall in Seneca, twelve miles away.

NIGHTLIFE

The Esso Club: This joint has been open for seventy-nine years. Yeah, it used to be an Esso gas station and kept the name and familiar logo sign. Drink specials abound, starting at lunchtime, and there's food, too. Of course, they also sell T-shirts and memorabilia. *129 Old Greenville Highway, Clemson, SC 29631, 864-654-5120, theessoclub.com*

Tiger Town Tavern: The joint opened in 1977 as a pool hall and beer-only joint. It's grown into the ultimate sports bar/watering hole with happy hour, pitcher specials, and trivia contests. The second story of the building is called Top of the Tavern, which opened in 1983. In 1994, Tiger Town opened a full-service kitchen and full bar. Now the patrons only have to go home to sleep. *364 College Ave., Clemson, SC 29631, 864-654-5901, www.tigertowntavern.com*

LAST-MINUTE TIPS

Where to Shop: If you're looking for the locally owned, university-themed group of stores, visit College Avenue. Think Marshall Street, with Clemson orange and purple instead of Syracuse's orange and blue.

Where to Buy Tickets: Major college sporting events always attract folks hawking tickets around the campus. You can also check stubhub.com and www.clemsontigers.com.

TRAVELING TO CLEMSON?

Clemson is about a forty-minute drive from the Greenville-Spartanburg International Airport and two hours from the more-affordable Atlanta International Airport. Driving time from Syracuse to Clemson is about thirteen hours.

Duke

Duke University traces its origins through several name changes and one relocation. In 1838, Methodist and Quaker families started a school in Randolph County. The school became known as Union Institute. As the Quakers eventually sought their own school, Union was rechartered in 1851 as Normal College. In 1859, after the school's trustees agreed to offer free education for Methodist preachers in return for financial support from the church, the name was changed to Trinity College.

In 1892, Washington Duke, a former Confederate soldier who had made a fortune in the tobacco business, gave $85,000 to Trinity College, which enabled the Methodist school in North Carolina's Randolph County to move to Durham. Later, Duke bestowed more than $300,000 to Trinity.

In 1924, Duke's son, James B. Duke, established The Duke Endowment, a $40 million trust fund, part of which was used to build a university around Trinity College. A project to renovate the school's old campus and create a new one cost $19 million. The school's president pushed to change Trinity's name to Duke University.

DUKE UNIVERSITY

STUDENTS
6,504

DURHAM
pop. 233,252

WALLACE WADE STADIUM
33,941

CAMERON INDOOR STADIUM
9,314

COLORS
Duke Blue & White

NICKNAME
Blue Devils

MASCOT
Blue Devil

CAMPUS ATTRACTIONS
Duke University Chapel, Sarah P. Duke Gardens, Nasher Museum of Art

PHONE
919-684-8111
(general information)

919-684-2444
(campus police)

919-684-2120
(athletic department)

TICKETS
919-681-2583 or
www.goduke.com

Intercollegiate athletics has always played a large role at Duke; even before it was Duke. On November 27, 1888, Trinity contested North Carolina in one of the earliest college football games played in the South. Trinity's 16-0 victory came on Thanksgiving Day. Trinity's first basketball game was against Wake Forest on March 2, 1906. Wake Forest won 24-10.

Duke joined the Southern Conference in 1924 and remained a member until leaving for the Atlantic Coast Conference in 1953. While Duke is currently known as a basketball school, its early successes came on the gridiron. Legendary coach Wallace Wade guided Duke to nine Southern Conference titles and two Rose Bowl appearances.

The 1938 team was unbeaten, untied, and unscored upon as it prepared to play Southern California in the Rose Bowl on January 2, 1939. A fourth-quarter field goal gave Duke a 3-0 lead, but USC's fourth-string quarterback came on to throw a game-winning touchdown with forty seconds remaining.

On January 1, 1942, Duke took part in the most unusual Rose Bowl ever. After the Japanese bombed Pearl Harbor, large crowds were not permitted to gather on the West Coast so the Rose Bowl was moved to Durham, where No. 2 Duke took on No. 12 Oregon State. The Beavers upset Duke, 20-16, in the only time the Rose Bowl has ever been played outside Pasadena, California.

Duke has played in just six bowl games since then, but the school's basketball program has become a national powerhouse. Fans who are new to the ACC should know that long before Christian Laettner and Bobby Hurley, there was Dick Groat and Jack Marin, and before Mike Krzyzewski, there was Bill Foster, and before him Vic Bubas.

Bubas coached the Blue Devils from 1960 to 1969, compiling a .761 winning percentage. Bubas's teams advanced to the NCAA Final Four in 1963, 1964, and 1966. In 1978, Foster guided a Duke team that featured Mike Gminski and Gene Banks to the NCAA final. The Blue Devils lost 94-88 to Kentucky.

Krzyzewski, a Bob Knight disciple who had played and coached at Army, took over as Duke's head coach in 1980. Duke suffered two losing seasons in Krzyzewski's first three years, but the Blue Devils would soon become synonymous with NCAA Tournament success.

The 1986 team advanced to the NCAA championship game, where the Blue Devils lost to Louisville. Duke went back to the Final Four again in 1988, 1989, and 1990. The Blue Devils finally claimed their first national title in 1991

Football

NATIONAL CHAMPIONSHIPS (0): The 1938 Duke football team was undefeated, untied, and unscored upon during the regular season. On January 2, 1939, the third-ranked Blue Devils played No. 7 Southern California in the Rose Bowl. The Blue Devils led 3-0 after Tony Ruffa's field goal with fourteen minutes in the fourth quarter. But with forty seconds remaining in the game, Doyle Nave, USC's fourth-string quarterback, threw a sixteen-yard touchdown pass to Al Krueger.

ACC CHAMPIONSHIPS (7): 1953, 1954, 1955, 1960, 1961, 1962, 1989

BOWL RECORD: 3-5 (.375). Last bowl—34-20 loss to Wisconsin in 1995 Hall of Fame Bowl

LONGEST WINNING STREAK: 11 games (twice), 1932-33, 1940-41

WINNINGEST COACH: Wallace Wade (1931-41, 1946-50), 110-36-7 (.742)

HEISMAN TROPHY WINNERS OR HIGHEST HEISMAN FINISH: Running back Ace Parker, 6th in 1936

Basketball

NATIONAL CHAMPIONSHIPS (4): 1991, 1992, 2001, 2010

ACC REGULAR SEASON CHAMPIONSHIPS (19): 1954, 1958, 1963, 1964, 1965, 1966, 1979, 1986, 1991, 1992, 1994, 1997, 1998, 1999, 2000, 2001, 2004, 2006, 2010

ACC TOURNAMENT CHAMPIONSHIPS (19): 1960, 1963, 1964, 1966, 1978, 1980, 1986, 1988, 1992, 1999, 2000, 2001, 2002, 2003, 2005, 2006, 2009, 2010, 2011

NCAA TOURNAMENT RECORD: 102-34 (.750) Last appearance—Lost 85-63 to Louisville in the Elite 8 of the 2013 tournament.

WINNINGEST COACH: Mike Krzyzewski (1981-present), 854-232 (.786)

NATIONAL PLAYERS OF THE YEAR: Nine Duke players have been named National Player of the Year—Dick Groat (1952), Art Heyman (1963), Johnny Dawkins (1986), Danny Ferry (1989), Christian Laettner (1992), Elton Brand (1999), Shane Battier (2001), Jason Williams (2001, 2002), J.J. Redick (2005, 2006)

as a team led by Laettner and Hurley defeated UNLV in the final. Duke won again the following year, becoming the first school in nineteen years to win back-to-back titles. Since then, Krzyzewski's teams have returned to the Final Four five times, winning everything in 2001 and 2010. Aside from his four NCAA titles, Krzyzewski has also become the NCAA's all-time winningest coach, surpassing his former coach and mentor, Bob Knight, along the way.

LEGENDS

Ace Parker
One of the greatest players in Duke history, Ace Parker earned All-American honors in both 1935 and 1936. In his three years at Duke, the Blue Devils posted a 24-5 record. Parker also played professional football for the Brooklyn Dodgers and Boston Yanks. He was the NFL's Most Valuable Player in 1940. A tremendous all-around athlete, Parker played pro baseball with the Philadelphia Athletics. He is enshrined in both the College and Pro Football Halls of Fame.

Sonny Jurgensen
Many people know Sonny Jurgensen's name, but they don't remember that the Hall of Fame quarterback played at Duke. That's partly because his pro career might have been better than his college career. Jurgensen, a native of Wilmington, N.C., played at Duke from 1954 to 1956, spending time at both defensive back and quarterback. He was a fourth-round draft choice of the Philadelphia Eagles. His best years in the NFL were in Washington, where he helped the Redskins to four playoff appearances. After a seventeen-year pro career, Jurgensen was inducted into the Pro Football Hall of Fame in 1983.

Christian Laettner
In his Duke career, Laettner was a member of four Final Four and two national championship teams. In 1991, he led Duke to its first national title, and then the Blue Devils won again in 1992. His last-second shot against Kentucky in the East Region finals of the 1992 tournament remains one of the most iconic moments in NCAA history. He was named National Player of the Year in 1992.

Dick Groat

One of the finest athletes of all-time, Groat played both basketball and baseball at Duke from 1949 to 1952. As a junior, he led the nation in scoring. He was named the National Player of the Year as a senior. He was also a first-team All-American in baseball and led the Blue Devils to the College World Series. He was selected in the first round of the 1952 NBA draft but went onto a fourteen-year career in the Major Leagues, earning the 1960 National League MVP award and winning World Series titles with the Pittsburgh Pirates and St. Louis Cardinals. Groat is currently the color commentator for the Pittsburgh Panthers basketball team.

STADIUM

Wallace Wade Stadium: Duke Stadium opened in the fall of 1929. In the first game at the stadium, Duke suffered a 52-7 loss to Pittsburgh. In 1967, Duke officials renamed the stadium Wallace Wade Stadium in honor of the man who guided the Blue Devils to two Rose Bowls and whose 110 coaching victories remains a school record.

NOTABLE ALUMS

Elizabeth Dole
U.S. senator, commissioner of the Federal Trade Commission, U.S. secretary of transportation, U.S. secretary of labor, president of the American Red Cross

Richard Nixon
37th president of the United States

William DeVries
the first doctor to perform a successful permanent artificial heart implant

John Feinstein
award-winning sports writer, best-selling author

ARENA

Cameron Indoor Stadium: According to legend, Eddie Cameron and Wallace Wade sketched out the first plans for Duke's Indoor Stadium on a matchbook cover. Cameron holds just 9,000 fans, making it one of the smallest arenas at a major college campus; however, the building was originally to be big. When Duke officials asked for a capacity of 8,000, the architects argued against such a large number, pointing out that Yale's new basketball facility seated just 1,600. The school officials got their wish. The Indoor Stadium opened in 1940. The building's name was changed to Cameron Indoor Stadium in 1972 to honor Duke's longtime athletic director and former basketball coach Eddie Cameron. His name and the name of the gym has been adopted by Duke's famous student section, the Cameron Crazies.

CUSE CONNECTION

ALL-TIME FOOTBALL RECORD VS. SYRACUSE: 2-0

1938: Duke 21, Syracuse 0 (Syracuse)

1939: Duke 33, Syracuse 6 (Durham)

ALL-TIME BASKETBALL RECORD VS. SYRACUSE: 2-2

1966: Duke 91, Syracuse 81 (Raleigh, N.C., NCAA Tournament)

1971: Syracuse 74, Duke 72 (Madison Square Garden)

1989: Syracuse 78, Duke 76 (Greensboro, N.C.)

1998: Duke 80, Syracuse 67 (Tampa, Fla., NCAA Tournament)

Greg Paulus: Paulus grew up in the Syracuse area and attended Christian Brothers Academy, where he starred in both football and basketball. He was recruited by Syracuse and Notre Dame but eventually decided to play basketball at Duke. After completing his career at Duke, Paulus took advantage of an NCAA rule that allows student-athletes to use their fifth year to play a different sport at another school. Paulus returned home to Syracuse, where he became the starting quarterback for the Orange in the 2009 season.

The U.S. Olympic team: After the United States men's basketball team lost three games on its way to a bronze medal in the 2004, a different approach was needed. Jerry Colangelo, the director of USA Basketball, convinced Duke coach Mike Krzyzewski to become the head coach of the U.S. Olympic team and then asked Syracuse coach Jim Boeheim, who was also the chairman of the USA Selection Committee, to be his top assistant. Krzyzewski and Boeheim combined to lead the USA to gold medals in both the 2008 and 2012 Olympics.

Michael Gbinije: Most conferences have rules prohibiting student-athletes from transferring to another school within the conference. Michael Gbinije played at Duke during the 2011-12 season. He then transferred to Syracuse, which at the time was still a member of the Big East Conference. Gbinije, who sat out the 2012-13 season according to NCAA rules, still has three years of eligibility remaining, and he will play all of those in the ACC as Syracuse enters the conference for the 2013-14 season. Duke coach Mike Krzyzewski approved Gbinije's transfer to Syracuse, in part because of his long-standing association with SU's Jim Boeheim.

MASCOT

Duke traces the roots of its Blue Devils nickname back to World War I. The *Chasseurs Alpins*, a special unit of French soldiers, had become known as "*les Diables Bleus*" for their distinctive blue uniforms complete with cape and beret. At the end of the war, Trinity College's student newspaper held a contest to find a nickname for the school's football team, which had several unofficial nicknames, including the Methodists and the Trinity Eleven. Blue Devils earned the nomination but was eventually rejected because the use of Devils was feared to be too controversial for the Methodist school. In 1922, student leaders, including editors at the student newspaper, took it upon themselves to use the Blue Devils nickname. The expected opposition never came and the Blue Devils nickname has been around ever since.

"Fight! Blue Devils, Fight!"

Fight! Fight, Blue Devils

Fight for Duke and the Blue and White

March on through

For the touchdown's there for you,

Go get 'em!

Duke is out to win today,

Carolina goodnight!

So, turn on the steam, team,

Fight! Blue Devils, fight!

OTHER SPORTS

While known mainly for men's basketball, Duke has a very strong athletic program. The women's golf team has won five NCAA championships. The women's tennis team has reached the NCAA Final Four seven times and won its first national title in 2009. The women's lacrosse team has made five Final Four appearances. Men's soccer (1986) and men's lacrosse (2010) have both won NCAA titles.

GAME DAY

MEDIA

Broadcasting the Game: WDNC-AM 620 and WKIX-FM 102.9 in Durham

Covering the Blue Devils: www.heraldsun.com (*Durham Morning-Herald*), www.newsobserver.com (*Raleigh News & Observer*)

TAILGATING

The most fun prior to a Duke game can be found in Blue Devil Alley, which is located outside the north gate of Wallace Wade Stadium near Card Gym and Cameron Indoor Stadium. This area features interactive games, entertainment, and food. Blue Devil Alley opens two and a half hours before each game. During basketball season, this same area becomes known as Krzyzewskiville, as it is where Duke students camp out for basketball games.

Families with children will want to check out the Coca-Cola Kids' Zone inside Wallace Wade Stadium. The zone has inflatable games, face-painting, and other activities. The Kids' Zone opens two hours before kickoff.

SHUTTLE

There are shuttles from the general public courtesy shuttle lots. The cost to park in these lots is ten dollars. Most general public parking lots open four hours prior to kickoff. Two lots open at 7 a.m. on game days. These are the Chemistry Lot located on Circuit Drive and the Jogging Trail Lot located at N.C. 751 and Cameron Boulevard.

The walking times from the general parking lots range anywhere from six minutes to fifteen minutes.

TRADITIONS

The Blue Devil Walk: Two hours before each home game, the Duke football team takes part in the Blue Devil Walk. The walk starts at the Duke Chapel and courses its way through Blue Devil Alley and Cameron Indoor Stadium until the team arrives at Wallace Wade Stadium. Fans can line up and watch the players as they walk to the stadium.

The Cameron Crazies: The Duke student section at Cameron Indoor Stadium has become famous (or infamous, depending on your point of view) for its loud support of the Blue Devils basketball team. At times inventive and clever, the Cameron Crazies have come under fire on occasion for crossing the line of decency and good sportsmanship. Regardless, the Crazies can raise a ruckus inside the Blue Devils' band-box of a gym, creating an incredibly hostile environment for visiting teams.

ABOUT TOWN

Durham, which got its name in 1853, began as a town built on tobacco, specifically brightleaf tobacco. This variation of tobacco was the foundation for Washington Duke and his family. It gave rise to one of the world's largest corporations, whose umbrella included American Tobacco, Liggett & Myers,

R.J. Reynolds, and P. Lorillard. But Durham is also known as the City of Medicine with over 300 medical and health-related companies. The 1950s and 1960s saw the rise of Research Triangle Park, which now consists of more than 140 major research and development companies.

LODGING

Washington Duke Inn: The Washington Duke Inn & Golf Club is located right on the Duke campus. As the name suggests, the hotel is situated on the Duke University golf course. It rests on 300 acres with 271 guest rooms and suites. *3001 Cameron Blvd., Durham, NC 27705, 800-443-3853 or 919-490-0999, www.washingtondukeinn.com*

Marriott Durham Convention Center: This Marriott, which was renovated in 2008, is located in Durham's historic downtown. The property is adjacent to the renowned Carolina Theatre. Duke University is less than three miles away. *201 Foster St., Durham, NC 27701, 919-768-6000 or 800-909-8375, www.marriott.com/hotels/travel/rducv-durham-marriott-city-center*

Morehead Manor Bed & Breakfast: For travelers looking for a quiet, elegant stay while in the Durham, the Morehead Manor offers all that plus proximity to Durham's downtown area, the Durham Athletic Park, and Brightleaf Square. The Colonial Revival–style home, which was originally built for the CEO of Liggett & Myers, now offers four guest bedrooms. *914 Vickers Ave., Durham, NC 27701, 919-687-4366 or 888-437-6333, www.moreheadmanor.com*

EATING

The Original Q-Shack: The Q-Shack offers a splendiferous array of pork, ribs, brisket, chicken, turkey, and sausage. They smoke all the meats right in-house. And there's even a special menu (for pick-up only) to stock your pre-game tailgating parties. *2510 University Dr., Durham, NC 27707, 919-942-4BBQ, www.theqshackoriginal.com*

Broad Street Café: If you want good food along with good music at a great price, the Broad Street Café is your destination. Almost everything on the menu—from the wood-fired pizza to the baked desserts—is made in-house. And there's live music five nights a week. *1116 Broad St., Durham, NC 27705, 919-416-9707, www.thebroadstreetcafe.com*

Watts Grocery: The menu at Watts Grocery takes you right back to chef Amy Tournquist's kitchen. From the roasted pork shank over grits to the cornmeal-dusted flounder over Sea Island Pea Hoppin' John, this is down-home cooking at its finest. *1116 Broad St., Durham, NC 27705, 919-416-5040, www. wattsgrocery.com*

SIGHTSEEING

Duke Chapel: The classic Gothic structure is the heart of the Duke community. Construction began in 1930 and was finished two years later. The chapel continues as a place of worship, but tours are available. *401 Chapel Dr., Durham, NC 27708, 919-681-9488, chapel.duke.edu*

Duke Basketball Museum and Hall of Fame: In 2010, the Duke Basketball Museum and Hall of Fame opened in the Schwartz/Butters Athletic Center, which is located adjacent to Cameron Indoor Stadium. *306 Towerview Rd., Durham, NC 27708, 919-613-7500*

Historic Durham Athletic Park: Sports fans and movie buffs will want to visit Durham Athletic Park, the site where *Bull Durham* was filmed. It's located close to Duke's West Campus. *500 Corporation St., Durham, NC 27701, 919-687-6500, www.durhamathleticpark.com*

SHOPPING

Ninth Street Shopping District: For a uniquely Durham shopping experience, head to this eclectic district located two blocks west of Duke's East Campus. There are restaurants and shops of all sorts.

Duke Stores: Duke University Stores has everything Duke-related for your shopping needs. There are sixteen retail locations on the Duke campus, but the largest is the University Store. *106 Science Dr., Durham, NC 27708, 919-684-2344, www.dukestores.duke.edu*

NIGHTLIFE

The Tavern: Located near the Duke campus and Durham's 9th Street District, the Tavern offers an array of brews, billiards, darts, and flat-screen TVs. The menu is highlighted by a half-pound Angus burger, and the kitchen is open until 2 a.m. Thursday through Saturday. *1900 W. Markham Ave., Durham, NC 27705, 919-286-POOL (7665), www.thetaverndurham.com*

Motorco Music Hall: Motorco is in downtown Durham's Central Park district. It's within easy walking distance of several restaurants. Motorco derives its name from a former car dealership, and it's now Durham's largest music venue. Motorco regularly books national bands as well as the region's best performers. *723 Rigsbee Ave., Durham, NC 27701, 919-901-0875, motorcomusic.com*

Satisfaction Restaurant & Bar: Satisfaction has been doing business as a neighborhood sports bar since 1982. There are sixteen brews on tap and a huge selection of eighty-four bottled beers. The sports fan will love the twenty-eight high-definition TVs. *905 W. Main St., Suite 37, Durham, NC 27701, 919-682-7397, www.satisfactionrestaurant.com*

LAST-MINUTE TIPS

Where to Shop: The Streets at Southpoint (*6910 Fayetteville Road, I-40 Exit 276, Durham*) is a super-regional mall with an outdoor plaza called Main Street. There are more than 170 shops and restaurants plus a sixteen-screen cinema. *USA Today* included the Streets at Southpoint in its "10 great places to spend it all in one place."

Where to Buy Tickets: Duke football games rarely sell out. Tickets are usually available through the university's website (*www.godukes.com*) or at the box office. Basketball games are obviously more difficult.

TRAVELING TO DURHAM?

It takes less than half an hour to drive from Raleigh-Durham International Airport to the Duke campus. The Raleigh-Durham airport serves the Research Triangle area with a host of airlines. It's about a two-and-a-half-hour drive from Charlotte to Durham. The drive from Syracuse to Durham is just under eleven hours.

Florida State

Florida State University opened its doors to students in 1857 as the State Seminary West of the Suwannee River. Actually, the university can trace its beginnings back to 1823 when the Territorial Legislature began planning a system of higher education. Over twenty years later, following Florida's admission as a state, Congress granted two townships for the purpose of higher educational institutions. One was to be located east of the Suwannee River and the other to the west.

In 1856, Francis Eppes, the mayor of Tallahassee and the grandson of Thomas Jefferson, offered land and building for one of the two educational institutions. His bid was accepted. One year after the West Florida Seminary began operations, it became a coed institution after incorporating the Tallahassee Female Academy. The school's original site was on the same hill where FSU's Westcott Building is located.

In 1863, the school's name was changed to the Florida Military and Collegiate Institute, which is indicative of the addition of a military section for the training of cadets. Many of the cadets from the school fought in the Civil War. After the war, the school began growing into a formal post-secondary

FLORIDA STATE UNIVERSITY

STUDENTS
40,838

TALLAHASSEE
pop. 181,376

DOAK CAMPBELL STADIUM
82,300

DONALD L. TUCKER CENTER
12,200

COLORS
Garnet and Gold

NICKNAME
Seminoles

MASCOT
Chief Osceola and Renegade

CAMPUS ATTRACTIONS
Westcott Building,
Unconquered statue,
The Gates,
The FSU Arch

PHONE
850-644-6200
(general information)

850-644-1234
(campus police)

850-644-1403
(athletic department)

TICKETS
850-644-1830 or
www.seminoles.com

educational institutional. By 1897, it had become the first liberal arts college in the state of Florida. In 1901, the name changed again to Florida State College.

Athletics had begun to take hold at Florida State College. The football team captured the state championship in 1902, 1903, and 1905. But in 1905, the Florida State Legislature reorganized its higher education system. The University of Florida, located in Gainesville, was designated as the men's college, while the Florida State College in Tallahassee became a women's school. In 1909, the school's official name was changed to Florida State College for Women to reflect its all-female student body.

At the end of World War II, the return of thousands of veterans increased enrollment at Florida's colleges. In 1947, Florida State College for Women became coed and was named Florida State University. On October 18, 1947, Florida State lost to Stetson, 14-6, in the school's first football game since 1905.

The very next season, Florida State's football team went 7-1 under new coach Don Veller. The 1949 team put together a 9-1 record. And in 1950, Doak Campbell Stadium opened and the Seminoles went 8-0. Since then, Florida State has enjoyed many successful campaigns under coaches Bill Peterson, Bobby Bowden, and Jimbo Fisher. In 1964, Peterson guided the "Seven Magnificents" to a 9-1-1 record that included FSU's first win ever over Florida. That team featured standout receiver Fred Biletnikoff, who was FSU's first All-American.

In 1976, Bowden arrived from West Virginia. He took over a Seminoles team that had gone 4-29 in its previous three seasons. Bowden spent thirty-four years as FSU's head coach, guiding the Seminoles to 316 wins, 33 bowl appearances, 20 bowl victories, and two national championships. Florida State's history offers a pantheon of outstanding players, including Derrick Brooks, Charlie Ward, Deion Sanders, and Chris Weinke. Since joining the ACC in 1992, FSU has won thirteen conference championships. The Seminoles won national championships in 1993 and 1999.

Florida State's basketball program started with the 1947-48 season. The following year, Florida State joined the Dixie Conference. The school played in the Florida Intercollegiate Conference from 1954 to 1957 and then remained independent until joining the Metro Conference in 1976.

Florida State's first postseason appearance came in the 1968 NCAA Tournament. That year's team was led by All-American center Dave Cowens. The Seminoles went 19-8 before losing to Tennessee State in the first round of the NCAA Tournament.

Football

NATIONAL CHAMPIONSHIPS (2): 1993, 1999

ACC CHAMPIONSHIPS (13): 1992, 1993, 1994, 1995, 1996, 1997, 1998, 1999, 2000, 2002, 2003, 2005, 2012

BOWL RECORD: 25-14-2 (.641). Last bowl—31-10 over Northern Illinois in the 2013 Orange Bowl

LONGEST WINNING STREAK: 16 games (twice), 1990-91, 1992-93

WINNINGEST COACH: Bobby Bowden (1976-2009), 316-97-4 (.757)

HEISMAN TROPHY WINNERS (2): Quarterback Charlie Ward in 1993 and quarterback Chris Weinke in 2000

Basketball

NATIONAL CHAMPIONSHIPS (0): The 1971-72 team lost to UCLA in the national championship game.

ACC REGULAR SEASON CHAMPIONSHIPS (0): Florida State finished second in its first two years in the ACC, but since the 1993 season the Seminoles' best finish has been third.

ACC TOURNAMENT CHAMPIONSHIPS (1): 2012

NCAA TOURNAMENT RECORD: 15-14 (.517) Last appearance—Lost 62-56 to Cincinnati in the second round of the 2012 tournament.

WINNINGEST COACH: J.K. Kennedy (1948-1966), 236-208 (.532)

NATIONAL PLAYERS OF THE YEAR OR HIGHEST FINISH: Dave Cowens was a second-team All-America in 1970

The next time Florida State appeared in the NCAA Tournament, the Seminoles had a lot more success. The 1971-72 team, coached by Hugh Durham and featuring Ron King and Reggie Royals, advanced to the NCAA championship game. The Seminoles defeated Minnesota, Kentucky, and North Carolina before losing to UCLA in the finals. That team remains the most successful in school history. Since then, Florida State has reached the NCAA's Elite 8 just once (in 1993), but a host of great players have worn the garnet and gold, including Bob Sura, Al Thornton, Sam Cassell, Toney Douglas, and Doug Edwards.

In 2012, after twenty years battling the Tobacco Road powers, FSU coach Leonard Hamilton's Seminoles defeated North Carolina and Duke on the way to the school's first ACC Tournament title.

LEGENDS

Deion Sanders
Deion Sanders is regarded as one of the best athletes of all time. He was a two-time All-American at FSU, winning the Jim Thorpe Award as a senior in 1988. His jersey has been retired, and he's one of the few players in FSU history to have his locker permanently sealed. In 2011, he was inducted into the NFL Hall of Fame and the College Football Hall of Fame. In addition to his standout NFL career, Sanders also played Major League Baseball.

Charlie Ward
Charlie Ward led the Seminoles to their first national championship in 1993. He also won the Heisman Trophy that year. He set nineteen school records and seven ACC records in his two years as a starter. His number was just the third in school history to be retired. A versatile athlete, Ward would go onto to play in the NBA.

Dave Cowens
Dave Cowens played at Florida State from 1968 to 1970 and is still regarded as the greatest player in school history. He led the Seminoles to their first NCAA Tournament appearance in 1968. As a senior, he would earn All-America honors. He averaged 18.9 points and 17.2 rebounds in his career. Cowens remains the school's career leader in rebounds. He was a first-round pick of the Boston Celtics and was the NBA's Rookie of the Year in 1971. He helped the Celtics to the NBA title in 1974 and 1976. He was inducted into the Basketball Hall of Fame in 1991.

Bob Sura

Bob Sura scored 2,130 points in his career as a Seminole. He is still the school's all-time leading scorer and the only player in school history to score 2,000 points. As a sophomore, Sura was the leading scorer on FSU's NCAA Elite 8 team. He was the ACC's Rookie of the Year in 1992. He would become the first player in FSU history to be named first-team All-ACC. The Cleveland Cavaliers selected Sura in the first round of the 1995 NBA draft.

ARENA

Donald L. Tucker Center: The Tallahassee-Leon County Civic Center opened in 1981. The facility, which was financed by the city of Tallahassee, cost $33.8 million to build. The arena's name was changed in 2004 to recognize Donald L. Tucker, a former speaker of the Florida House of Representatives and the Special Ambassador for the United States to the Dominican Republic. The Civic Center is only two blocks from the Capitol building and is just across the street from FSU's Law School and Center for Professional Development.

STADIUM

Doak Campbell Stadium: Florida State football debuted in 1947 on Centennial Field. In 1950, Doak Campbell Stadium, named after a former FSU president, opened with a capacity of 15,000. The cost to build the original stadium was $250,000. Expansions began almost immediately—to 19,000 in 1954 and 25,000 in 1961. By the end of the 1970s, the stadium's capacity had increased to 40,500. Former FSU coach Bobby Bowden's teams went 164-30-2 at Doak Campbell. Today, the stadium seats over 82,000 fans.

CUSE CONNECTION

ALL-TIME FOOTBALL RECORD VS. SYRACUSE: 5-1

Last meeting October 1, 2005: Florida State 38, Syracuse 14

ALL-TIME BASKETBALL RECORD VS. SYRACUSE: 1-3

Last meeting March 12, 1997: Florida State 82, Syracuse 67

Floyd Little's last home game: On November 12, 1966, Syracuse faced Florida State at Archbold Stadium. It was Syracuse's final home game of the season and, thus, it would be the final game at Archbold for one of the greatest players in Syracuse history—Floyd Little. Little rushed for 193 yards on 25 carries to lead Syracuse to a 37-21 victory. Little rushed for three touchdowns, each from 24 yards out, and also scored on a two-point conversion.

Ill-advised taunt: On October 5, 1991, the Syracuse Orangemen learned that it doesn't pay to get in Chief Osceola's way. Prior to No. 10 Syracuse's game against No. 1 Florida State, the Syracuse players ran to midfield as Chief Osceola performed his pre-game ritual. Their act nearly incited a brawl. What happened instead was a beating. Syracuse jumped out to a 14-7 lead as Qadry Ismail caught a forty-four-yard touchdown pass and then returned a kickoff ninety-five yards for a score. After that, however, the Seminoles dominated, gaining 642 yards of total offense en route to a 46-14 victory. Florida State quarterback Casey Weldon, that year's Heisman Trophy runner-up, threw for 347 yards and three touchdowns.

Moten's first start: Lawrence Moten finished his career as Syracuse's all-time leading scorer, but he began his freshman year on the bench. In the third game of the 1991-92 season, Syracuse went up against Florida State in the ACC/Big East Challenge in Atlanta. Adrian Autry had a sprained ankle and couldn't start. Syracuse coach Jim Boeheim thought about starting sophomore Scott McCorkle, but decided to go with Moten. Moten scored eighteen points to lead Syracuse to an 89-71 upset of a Florida State team that featured Sam Cassell and Doug Edwards.

Leonard Hamilton and the Big East: Syracuse and Florida State may have played each other just four times, but Florida State coach Leonard Hamilton has plenty of experience against the Cuse. In the nine years of his ten-year run as the head coach at Miami, Hamilton's Hurricanes were members of the Big East Conference. From 1991 to 2000, Miami went 4-11 against Syracuse under Hamilton. Oddly, the two schools never faced each other in the Big East Tournament.

MASCOT

Prior to every Florida State home game, Chief Osceola, carrying a flaming spear, rides to midfield on an Appaloosa horse named Renegade. Upon arriving at midfield, Osceola plants the spear in the FSU logo. The tradition started on September 16, 1978, in a game against Oklahoma State. The original Osceola and Renegade were Jim Kidder and Reo. The horses are trained in the Renegade training program. The clothing and rigging that Osceola and Renegade use were designed and approved by the Seminole Indian Tribe of Florida.

"FSU Fight Song"

You've got to fight, fight, fight, for FSU

You've got to scalp 'em Seminoles;

You've got to win, win, win, win, win this game

And roll on down and make those goals

For FSU is on the warpath now,

and at the battle's end she's great

So fight, fight, fight, fight to victory,

our Seminoles from Florida State.

OTHER SPORTS

Florida State has won thirteen national championships. The women's softball program won back-to-back AIAW titles in 1981 and 1982. The golf program won the AIAW championship in 1981. But Florida State might be best known for its track teams. The women's team won the 1984 NCAA outdoor and the 1985 indoor championships. The men's team won the NCAA's outdoor title in 2006 and 2008 and then finished second in both 2009 and 2011.

GAME DAY

MEDIA

Broadcasting the Game: WTNY-FM 94.9 and WNLS-AM 1270 in Tallahassee, WHOO-AM 1080 in Orlando, WFTL-AM 850 in Miami

Covering the Seminoles: www.tallahassee.com (*Tallahassee Democrat*), www.orlandosentinel.com (*Orlando Sentinel*)

TAILGATING

Most of the lots surrounding Doak Campbell Stadium are reserved for Florida State athletic boosters. Tailgating is allowed in most lots, including the motorhome lot. The reserved lots open five hours prior to kickoff. For more information on game-day parking as well as tailgating, contact the parking director at 850-645-2533.

SHUTTLE

The Spirit Express and Dial-a-Ride will continue to provide shuttle services but the new parking and pick up location is at parking garage number 5 located at the corner of Pensacola Street and Copeland Street. Shuttles run beginning two hours prior to kickoff and run for up to an hour after the end of the game. Drop off and pick-up at Doak Campbell Stadium is located at Gate H in the bus loop. There is a nominal fee to park and ride.

TRADITIONS

War Chant: The familiar "war chant" goes back to the 1960s when the Marching Chiefs band would chant the melody of an FSU cheer. In 1984, during a Florida State football game against Auburn, the Marching Chiefs began their chant when some students sitting behind the band took up the cheer after the band had stopped. Soon thereafter, the familiar tomahawk chop started accompanying the chant. By 1986, the FSU War Chant had turned into a full-fledged phenomenon.

Sod games: Florida State's Sod Cemetery is the burial ground for chunks of turf from Florida State's biggest road victories. The tradition started in 1962 as FSU prepared to play Georgia at Sanford Stadium. Dean Coyle Moore, a longtime professor and member of FSU's athletic board, challenged the Seminoles to "bring back some sod from between the hedges at Georgia." Florida State beat Georgia, 18-0, and team captain Gene McDowell pulled up a piece of grass, which he presented to Moore at the next practice. Sod games are any road game in which FSU is the underdog, any game at Florida, ACC championship games, and bowl games.

ABOUT TOWN

Tallahassee traces its roots to the Creek (or Seminole) and Apalachee Indian nations, dating back nearly 10,000 years. Spanish colonists entered the region in the 1500s. In 1538, Spanish conquistador Hernando de Soto is believed to have observed the first Christmas in the continental United States near the

FIGHT, FIGHT, FIGHT
FOR FSU

current site of the Florida State Capitol. Tallahassee became Florida's capital in 1824, three years after Florida earned its statehood. Tallahassee was selected after the capital alternated between Pensacola and St. Augustine. Tallahassee, with a population of 181,376, has a vibrant arts community in addition to its government- and education-based populations.

LODGING

Governors Inn: This boutique hotel is conveniently located in downtown Tallahassee, close to the capitol and the Leon County Civic Center. Some rooms overlook a courtyard, others include four-poster beds, and there are loft suites with fireplaces. The hotel also offers special rates for football weekends. *209 South Adams St., Tallahassee, FL 32301, 850-681-6855, www. thegovinn.org*

Little English Guesthouse: This distinctive English-style hotel is the only Bed & Breakfast in the capitol area. It's located just ten minutes from the FSU campus and about twenty minutes from the airport. The décor includes pieces from the owner's childhood in England. *737 Timberlane Rd., Tallahassee, FL 32312, 850-907-9777, www.littleenglishguesthouse.com*

Sheraton Four Points: If you're looking for a traditional hotel close to the game, the Sheraton Four Points in downtown Tallahassee will do the trick. The hotel lends bicycles to guests who want to tour the FSU campus or you can relax by the saline pool at the outdoor bar. *316 West Tennessee St., Tallahassee, FL 32301, 850-422-0071, www.starwoodhotels.com*

EATING

Gordo's: Gordo's opened in 1996 and is a Tallahassee favorite. The Cuban-flavored menu includes croquetas, yuca, empanadas, maduros, and Cuban sandwiches plus burgers and salads. The Gordo fries are a must. There are a variety of beers or the adventurous can wash down their meal with a Gordo's Smash. *1907 West Pensacola St., Tallahassee, FL 32304, 850-576-5767. www. gordoscubanfood.com*

Nick's Café: Nick's is the oldest diner in Tallahassee and it's a local favorite. There's not much going for Nick's from the outside, but step inside and the aroma of fried chicken, fried catfish, and more fills the senses. There are mounted bass and football posters on the walls. Yankees who want to fit in should order the sweet tea. *1431 South Monroe St., Tallahassee, FL 32301, 850-222-0371*

Andrew's 228: Located downtown within a stone's throw of the state capitol, Andrew's consists of a bar and grill and the full-service restaurant. The burgers and sandwiches in the grill are named after famous politicos. The 228 Restaurant offers a blend of American and Italian cuisine. *228 South Adams St., Tallahassee, FL 32304, 850-222-3444, www.andrewsdowntown.com*

SIGHTSEEING

Mission San Luis: The historical site of the former Spanish and Indian village was first settled in 1656 and then abandoned in 1704. There are exhibits, reconstructions, and guided tours available. *2100 West Tennessee St., Tallahassee, FL 32304, 850-245-6406, www.missionsanluis.org*

Lake Jackson Mounds Archaeological State Park: Lake Jackson is located just north of Tallahassee. From 1050 to 1500, Native Americans inhabited the area. The current state park marks the site of what is now known as the Southeastern Ceremonial Complex. The park encompasses four earthen temple mounds, with two available for viewing by the public. The largest mound is 278 feet by 312 feet at the base and approximately 36 feet in height. *3600 Indian Mounds Rd., Tallahassee, FL 32303, 850-922-6007, www.floridastateparks.org/lakejackson*

SHOPPING

Bill's Bookstore: There are three Bill's Bookstore locations in Tallahassee, but the original sits across the street from the Main Gates to the FSU campus. On game days, FSU fans get war paint smeared on them by store employees. *111 South Copeland St., Tallahassee, FL 32304, 850-728-6676*

Railroad Square Art Park: Railroad Square is home to over fifty studios, galleries, and small locally owned shops. On the first Friday of each month, the Square hosts "First Friday Gallery Hop." There are musicians and a café built out of a real caboose. *567 Industrial Dr., Tallahassee, FL 32310, 850-224-1308, www.railroadsquare.com*

NIGHTLIFE

Bullwinkle's Saloon: Bullwinkle's is a Florida State University institution. It's more than just your typical college bar. There's a party every night with daily specials and live music of all kinds from reggae to indie rock. *620 W. Tennessee St., Tallahassee, FL 32304, 850-224-0651, www.bullwinklessaloon.com*

AJ Sports Bar: Arguably the best sports bar in a sports-mad town, AJ's is fitted with fifty HD TVs. Thirsty? There's the Big Daddy, a thirty-two-ounce beer in a frosty mug. There are two dance floors, live music, and karaoke. The owner is a Florida State grad, so make friends. *1800 West Tennessee St., Tallahassee, FL 32304, 850-681-0731, www.ajsportsbar.net*

Potbelly's and The Painted Lady: Potbelly's is a party place. A classic college bar located near the FSU campus. Right next door is The Painted Lady, an upscale nightclub. Both venues offer outdoor areas. *459 College Ave., Tallahassee, FL 32304, 850-224-2233, www.potbellys.net*

LAST-MINUTE TIPS

Where to Shop: Governor's Square Mall (1500 Apalachee Parkway) is located close to the FSU campus. The mall features four anchor stores plus specialty shops and eating options.

Where to Buy Tickets: Through digital ticketing, Florida State University has entered into the secondary ticket market. Fans using the Florida State Ticket Marketplace, which is now associated with stubhub.com, can be certain that the tickets they purchase are legitimate. For more information contact the FSU ticket office at ticketoffice@seminoles.com or call 1-888-FSU-Nole.

TRAVELING TO TALLAHASSEE?

Three major airlines— Delta, United, and American—serve the Tallahassee Regional Airport. Syracuse fans can fly to Tallahassee through Atlanta, Charlotte, and Washington, D.C. Tallahassee is located 160 miles west of Jacksonville on I-90 and 250 miles north of Orlando. If you're driving from Syracuse, start now. It's a little over 1,200 miles.

Georgia Tech

The idea behind Georgia Tech started in 1882 when Georgia state leaders proposed a school of technology as a way for the South to keep up with the Industrial Revolution taking place in the North.

In 1883, the Georgia General Assembly sent a group, including Georgia School of Technology founder Nathaniel Edwin Harris, on a tour of schools in the North. The committee returned with a model based on the Worcester (Massachusetts) Polytechnic Institute, which combined theory and practice as the core of its teachings.

The Georgia School of Technology was founded on October 13, 1885, in Atlanta. Its official opening came three years later after the construction of Tech Tower and a shop building. The site of the school was on a hill where fortifications had once protected Atlanta during the Civil War. By the turn of the century, the school was offering degrees in mechanical, electrical, civil, textile, and chemical engineering. In 1948, the name was changed to the Georgia Institute of Technology to reflect its evolution from an engineering school to a full technical and research institution.

Georgia Tech fielded its first football team in 1892; a rag-tag group of students known as the Blacksmiths who lost all three of their games. In 1893, Georgia Tech played Georgia for the first time. Georgia Tech won 28-6, registering the first victory in school history. After the game, Georgia fans, according to historical reports, threw stones at the Georgia Tech players. It was the spark to a rivalry that's come to be known as "Clean, Old-Fashioned Hate."

Georgia Tech's fortunes were scarce in the program's early days. Between 1897 and 1903, Georgia Tech won just four games. In 1903, Tech suffered a 73-0 loss to Clemson. After that season, Georgia Tech officials offered the coach at Clemson a job. His name was John Heisman. Heisman, the namesake for football's Heisman Trophy, turned Tech around. His first team went 8-1-1.

In 1916, Georgia Tech crushed Cumberland, 222-0, which remains the largest margin of victory in college football history. The reason for the massive blowout was a baseball game between the two schools the year prior. Cumberland, using professional players as ringers, defeated Tech 22-0. Heisman, angered by Cumberland's use of pro athletes, got his revenge on the football field.

In 1917, Georgia Tech went 9-0 and was named national champions. The team became known as the Golden Tornado. In 1928, Georgia Tech won its second national championship. By then the program was under the direction of William Alexander. The 1928 team was the first Georgia Tech squad to play in a bowl game. The 1929 Rose Bowl game against California is remembered for California center Roy Riegels mistakenly returning a fumble the wrong way, finally being tackled by his own teammates at the 3 yard line. Georgia Tech won 8-7 to finish 10-0. Georgia Tech also won national titles in 1952, under legendary coach Bobby Dodd, and 1990 with Bobby Ross at the helm.

The roots of the Georgia Tech basketball program intertwine with the football program. Georgia Tech began playing basketball in 1905-06. After not fielding a team in 1906-07, the school resumed playing under the direction of John Heisman. The football coaching icon guided the Tech basketball team for three seasons. William Alexander also coached basketball for four seasons.

Georgia Tech made its first NCAA Tournament appearance in 1960. The Yellow Jackets didn't return to the NCAAs until 1985. Georgia Tech has been a top-notch program over the past thirty years. The Yellow Jackets advanced to the Final Four in 1990 and the championship game in 2004. Players such as Mark Price, John Salley, Stephon Marbury, and Dennis Scott have lifted Georgia Tech's national profile.

Georgia Tech was a founding member of the Southern Intercollegiate

Football

NATIONAL CHAMPIONSHIPS (4): 1917, 1928, 1952, 1990

ACC CHAMPIONSHIPS (3): 1990, 1998, 2009

BOWL RECORD: 22-18 (.550). Last bowl—A 30-27 overtime loss to Utah in the 2011 Hyundai Sun Bowl

LONGEST UNDEFEATED STREAK: 31 games (1914 to 1918). Tech won the last two games in the 1914 season, went 7-0-1 the following year, 8-0-1 in 1916, undefeated and untied at 9-0 in 1917, and then won the first five games in 1918 before losing 32-0 to Pittsburgh. During the streak, Tech tied Georgia and Washington & Lee.

WINNINGEST COACH: Bobby Dodd (1945-66), 165-64-8 (.713)

HEISMAN TROPHY WINNERS OR HIGHEST HEISMAN FINISH: Quarterback Billy Lothridge, second in 1963; quarterback Joe Hamilton, second in 1999; running back Clint Castleberry, third in 1942

Basketball

NATIONAL CHAMPIONSHIPS (0): Georgia Tech lost to Connecticut in the 2004 NCAA title game. The Yellow Jackets also appeared in the 1990 Final Four.

ACC REGULAR SEASON CHAMPIONSHIPS (2): 1985, 1996

ACC TOURNAMENT CHAMPIONSHIPS (3): 1985, 1990, 1993

NCAA TOURNAMENT RECORD: 23-16 (.589) Last NCAA appearance—A 75-66 loss to Ohio State in the second round of the 2010 tournament.

WINNINGEST COACH: Bobby Cremins (1982-2000), 354-237 (.599)

NATIONAL PLAYERS OF THE YEAR: Dennis Scott in 1990

Athletic Association in 1895. In 1921, Georgia Tech joined fourteen other schools to start the Southern Conference. In 1931, Georgia Tech left the Southern Conference to form the Southeastern Conference. In 1964, Georgia Tech left the SEC to become an independent and remained so until helping to found the Metro-6 Conference in 1975. Georgia Tech joined the ACC in 1978.

LEGENDS

Clint Castleberry

In 1942, Clint Castleberry, a freshman running back, led Georgia Tech to a 9-2 record that included wins over nationally ranked Auburn and Alabama plus a win over Notre Dame. Castleberry finished third in the Heisman Trophy voting despite being a freshman. On January 1, 1943, Georgia Tech lost to Texas, 14-7, in the Cotton Bowl. It would be Castleberry's final game. After the season, he enlisted in the U.S. Army, and on November 7, 1944, he died in a plane crash off the coast of West Africa. His No. 19 remains the only retired jersey in Georgia Tech history.

Bobby Dodd

Bobby Dodd coached at Georgia Tech from 1945 to 1966. In those twenty-two seasons, Dodd's teams won 165 games and lost just 64. The 1952 team went undefeated and was named national champions. In 1993, Dodd was inducted into the College Football Hall of Fame. He had previously been inducted in 1959 on the merits of his playing career at the University of Tennessee. Dodd and Amos Alonzo Stagg are the only people inducted into the Hall of Fame as both player and coach.

Mark Price

Mark Price played at Georgia Tech from 1982 to 1986, finishing his career with 2,193 points. He won the ACC's Rookie of the Year Award in 1983. He was a three-time All-American and first-team honoree in 1985. He made the ACC's first-team three times, including his junior year when he was named the ACC's Player of the Year as a junior. He was also the ACC tournament MVP in 1985 while leading Tech to the tournament title.

Dennis Scott

Dennis Scott was the ACC's Rookie of the Year in 1988 and the ACC's Player of the Year in 1990, matching Mark Price's feat. Scott scored an ACC-record 970 points during the 1989-90 season. In 1990, he became the first and only Georgia Tech player to be named National Player of the Year.

STADIUM

Bobby Dodd Stadium: Georgia Tech's Bobby Dodd Stadium at Grant Field was built in 1913, making it the oldest on-campus football facility in Division I-A. The stadium was originally known as Grant Field. The original concrete stands, West Stands, were built by Georgia Tech students. The stands sat 5,600 fans. Stands on the opposite side of the field were completed in 1924 and more seating on the south end of the field was finished the following year, bringing Grant Field's capacity to 30,000.

More expansions followed over the years, but the facility remained known as Grant Field until 1988 when the Georgia State Board of Regents decided to add Bobby Dodd's name to the stadium. Dodd was Tech's legendary coach from 1945 to 1966, during which time the Yellow Jackets went 165-64-8 and played in thirteen bowl games.

NOTABLE ALUMS

Bobby Jones
Hall of Fame golfer, winner of golf's Grand Slam, designed the course at Augusta National, which is home to the Masters.

Jimmy Carter
Class of 1946. He was the thirty-ninth president of the United States. In 2002, he received the Nobel Peace Prize.

Cecil B. Day
Founder of the Days Inn hotel chain

John Young
NASA astronaut was part of several missions, including *Gemini 3*, *Gemini 10*, *Apollo 10*, and *Apollo 16*. Walked on the moon. First commander of the space shuttle.

ARENA

McCamish Pavilion: Georgia Tech moved into the McCamish Pavilion for the 2012-13 season. The Pavilion, which seats 8,900 fans, is built on the same site as Alexander Memorial Coliseum where Tech played from 1956 to 2011. In their final game at Alexander Coliseum, which was also known as the Thrillerdome, the Yellow Jackets defeated Miami 66-57 on March 6, 2011. Georgia Tech split the 2011-12 season between the Philips Arena, which is the home of the NBA's Atlanta Hawks, and the Arena at Gwinnett in Duluth, Georgia.

CUSE CONNECTION

ALL-TIME FOOTBALL RECORD VS. SYRACUSE: 2-0

2001: Georgia Tech 13, Syracuse 7 (Kickoff Classic in East Rutherford, N.J.)

2004: Georgia Tech 51, Syracuse 14 (Champs Bowl in Orlando)

ALL-TIME BASKETBALL RECORD VS. SYRACUSE: 2-2

1985: Georgia Tech 70, Syracuse 53 (NCAA Tournament, Atlanta)

2001: Georgia Tech 96, Syracuse 80 (Peach Bowl Classic, Atlanta)

2002: Syracuse 92, Georgia Tech 65 (Syracuse)

2010: Syracuse 80, Georgia Tech 76 (Legends Classic, Atlantic City)

Coach P's last game: On December 21, 2004, Syracuse and Georgia Tech, two teams sporting identical 6-5 records, met in the Champs Sports Bowl in Orlando. Syracuse coach Paul Pasqualoni had endured another season on the hot seat. Syracuse University athletic director Jake Crouthamel had just retired, but new athletic director Daryl Gross had voiced his support of Pasqualoni. But in the Champs Bowl, Georgia Tech roared out to a 35-6 halftime lead. The Yellow Jackets eventually won 51-14. The embarrassing loss sealed Pasqualoni's fate. He was dismissed eight days later.

George O'Leary: Now the head coach at Central Florida, George O'Leary cut his coaching teeth as an assistant at both Syracuse and Georgia Tech. O'Leary was the head coach at Liverpool (N.Y.) High School just outside of Syracuse from 1977 to 1979. He then became the defensive line coach at Syracuse. He stayed at Syracuse through the 1986 season before leaving to become defensive coordinator at Georgia Tech. He coached at Tech from 1987 to 1991, a stint that included the 1990 11-0-1 national championship season. He left Tech for a job with the San Diego Chargers but returned in 1994. He took over as head coach with three games remaining in the 1994 season. He would coach the Yellow Jackets from 1994 to 2001, compiling a 52-33 record and five bowl appearances.

Yellow Jacket-Orange links: Don Lowe was the coordinator of sports medicine at Syracuse for twenty-five years. He left SU in 2000 to become director of sports medicine at Georgia Tech, where he stayed until 2003. The training area at SU's Carmelo K. Anthony Basketball Center is named for Lowe and his wife, Mary . . . Syracuse's Derrick Coleman was the No. 1 pick in the 1990 NBA draft. Georgia Tech's Dennis Scott was the fourth player selected. . . . Syracuse's Carmelo Anthony and Georgia Tech's Chris Bosh were the No. 3 and 4 picks, respectively, in the 2003 NBA draft.

MASCOT

The Yellow Jacket nickname for Georgia Tech's athletic teams first surfaced in the *Atlanta Constitution* in 1905. At the time, newspaper references spelled the name "Yellowjackets." The term was actually used to describe Georgia Tech's supporters, many of whom wore bright yellow jackets.

Georgia Tech teams went by several other monikers before Yellow Jacket became the school's official nickname. Other nicknames included Engineers, Blacksmiths, Techs, and the Golden Tornado, a title given Coach John Heisman's national championship team in 1917 and used to describe Tech's best football teams until the late 1920s.

Georgia Tech's mascot, named Buzz, was a product of the nickname. The date of Buzz's origin is unknown.

"Ramblin' Wreck"

I'm a Ramblin' Wreck from Georgia Tech and a hell of an engineer,

A helluva, helluva, helluva, helluva, hell of an engineer,

Like all the jolly good fellows, I drink my whiskey clear,

I'm a Ramblin' Wreck from Georgia Tech and a hell of an engineer.

Oh, if I had a daughter, sir, I'd dress her in White and Gold,

And put her on the campus, to cheer the brave and bold.

But if I had a son, sir, I'll tell you what he'd do.

He would yell, "To Hell with Georgia," like his daddy used to do.

Oh, I wish I had a barrel of rum and sugar three thousand pounds,

A college bell to put it in and a clapper to stir it around.

I'd drink to all good fellows who come from far and near.

I'm a ramblin', gamblin', hell of an engineer.

GAME DAY

MEDIA

Broadcasting the Game: WQXI-AM 790 and WYAY-FM 106.7 in Atlanta

Covering the Yellow Jackets: www.ajc.com (*Atlanta Journal-Constitution*), www.nique.net (*The Technique*, student newspaper)

TAILGATING

Georgia Tech has few restrictions on tailgating. Fans are allowed to tailgate in Georgia Tech Athletic Association parking lots as long as the party doesn't take up another parking space. Most GTAA lots are sold out for the entire season. Permits are required. Some single-game permits are available at www.ramblinwreck.com. In addition, the GTAA sponsors a pre-game slate of activities known as Wreckfest. The event takes place at the north end of Bobby Dodd Stadium and starts about three hours before kickoff.

SHUTTLE

Fans can park at Atlantic Station and ride the Stinger Shuttle to the stadium. The shuttle starts two and a half hours before kickoff and continues until ninety minutes after the game. The shuttle picks up in front of Z Gallerie and drops off near the stadium. Atlantic Station offers a variety of restaurants and activities, including a conversion to TechTown on game days. For more information go to: www.atlanticstation.com.

OTHER SPORTS

Outside of football and basketball, two of the most successful athletic programs at Georgia Tech are baseball and men's golf. The baseball program is one of the best in the country. The Yellow Jackets appeared in the College World Series in 1994, 2002, and 2006. The program's alumni include Nomar Garciaparra, Mark Teixeira, Jason Varitek, and Matt Wieters. The golf team is a perennial participant in the NCAA championship, having gone for nine straight years. Golf legend Bobby Jones is a Georgia Tech graduate. More recently, *Golf Magazine* rated Georgia Tech as the No. 1 golf program in the country in 2005. The list of Georgia Tech alums who have played on the PGA Tour include Matt Kuchar, David Duval, and Stewart Cink.

TRADITIONS

Ramblin' Wreck: The Ramblin' Wreck is a 1930 Model A Ford Sport Coupe. The car has led the Georgia Tech football team onto the field prior to games since its debut on September 30, 1961, for a game against Rice. The Ramblin' Wreck tradition actually dates back to the 1920s when Dean of Students Floyd Field drove his 1914 Ford around campus. In later years, the university held a Ramblin' Wreck Parade during Homecoming festivities. The original Ramblin' Wreck was purchased in 1961 for $1,000.

Rat Caps: Visiting fans at a Georgia Tech football game will notice some students wearing gold-colored caps. The caps are referred to as Rat Caps. Members of Tech's freshman class are required to wear the caps and record the scores of Georgia Tech's games on the caps. The term "rat" is derived from the military description for a first-year student. The tradition began back in 1915 with the ANAK society, which honors juniors and seniors.

ABOUT TOWN

Located at the end of the Western & Atlantic railroad line, Atlanta was founded in 1837. The city's original name was Marthasville, in honor of the governor's daughter. It took on the nickname Terminus due to its location on the rail line. Finally, the name was changed to Atlanta in 1845. The name was chosen as the feminine version of Atlantic in the railroad's name. In 1864, Union general William Sherman burned Atlanta to the ground during his famous March to the Sea. Sherman's troops burned 70 percent of the city's buildings. Since then, Atlanta has become known for its rich social history, which includes the late Dr. Martin Luther King Jr. Today, Atlanta is a banking and entertainment hub. It's home to CNN and TBS and has hosted the Olympics, the Super Bowl, and the NCAA Final Four.

LODGING

The Glenn Hotel: A boutique hotel in the heart of downtown Atlanta, the Glenn is close to Centennial Olympic Park, the Georgia Aquarium, and World of Coca-Cola. It's affiliated with the Marriott chain. *110 Marietta St. NW, Atlanta, GA 30303, 404-521-2250, www.glennhotel.com*

Georgia Tech Hotel and Conference Center: Located in the Technology Square Complex on the Georgia Tech campus, the Georgia Tech Hotel boasts 252 rooms and suites. The hotel's business-oriented amenities and contemporary décor blend with its surroundings in the heart of Midtown Atlanta. *800 Spring St. NW, Atlanta, GA 30308, 404-347-9440, www.gatechhotel.com*

Hilton Garden Inn: Located in Atlanta's Luckie Marietta district, the hotel is well suited for sports fans who also want to be near the city's attractions. It's one block from the Georgia Aquarium and Centennial Olympic Park. The Georgia Tech campus is less than a mile away. *275 Baker St., Atlanta, GA 30313, 404-577-2001*

EATING

The Varsity: The world's largest drive-in restaurant has been serving its chili, onion rings, chili cheese dogs, and fried pies since 1928. Frank Gordy started the restaurant—one of Atlanta's most famous destinations. The Varsity sits on two acres and can accommodate 600 cars and 800 diners inside. It's estimated that 30,000 patrons visit the Varsity on days when Georgia Tech plays a home football game. *61 North Ave., Atlanta, GA 30308, 404-881-1706, www. thevarsity.com*

Engine 11 Firehouse Tavern: Built in 1906, Fire Station #11 was an active fire house for ninety years before being converted into one of the most unique restaurant/bars in Atlanta. It's located just blocks from the Georgia Tech campus. The menu consists of burgers, steaks, sandwiches, and the signature Chattahoochee chicken covered in melted Swiss and pimento cheeses. *30 North Ave., Atlanta, GA 30303, 404-873-FIRE (3473), www.engine11atl.com*

Antico Pizza: New Yorkers pride themselves on pizza, but Atlanta's got a little bit of Napoli in Antico Pizza. Owner Giovanni DiPalma is a master pizzaiolo, and his creations are traditional Pizza Napoletana. *1093 Hemphill Ave., Atlanta, GA 30318, 404-724-2333, www.anticopizza.it*

SIGHTSEEING

World of Coca-Cola: In 1886, Atlanta pharmacist Dr. John Pemberton created a syrupy soft drink that would become known as Coca-Cola. The World of Coca-Cola takes visitors through the soft drink's history and evolution. A unique must-see destination. *121 Baker St. NW, Atlanta, GA 30313, 404-676-5151 or 1-800-676-COKE (2653), www.worldofcoca-cola.com*

Centennial Olympic Park: The Olympic Park is located in downtown Atlanta. It was the hub of the 1996 Olympics. Today, the centerpiece of the park is the Fountain of Rings. While at the park, grab something to eat at Googie Burger. The World of Coca-Cola and the Georgia Aquarium are across the street. *404-223-4412, www.centennialpark.com*

Margaret Mitchell House: The home of the *Gone With the Wind* author is now a museum. The turn-of-the-century Tudor Revival building is listed on the National Register of Historic Places. It was built in 1899. Mitchell and her husband moved there in 1925. *990 Peachtree St., Atlanta, GA 30309, 404-249-7015, www.margaretmitchellhouse.com*

SHOPPING

Georgia Tech Bookstore: The official Georgia Tech campus bookstore has everything you'd ever want to wear in old gold and black. *48 5th Street, NW, Atlanta, GA 30308, 404-894-2515, www.gatech.bncollege.com*

Atlantic Station: Located close to the Tech campus, Atlantic Station boasts fifty retailers, a movie theater complex, and food options from pub fare to fine dining. *1380 Atlantic Dr., Suite 14250, Atlanta, GA 30363, 404-733-1221, www.atlanticstation.com*

NIGHTLIFE

Taco Mac: In 1979, some boys from Buffalo stopped in Atlanta on their way to Florida and decided to stay and open up a bar that would introduce Buffalo-style chicken wings to the South. They bought a Mexican restaurant named Taco Mac and before they had enough money to buy a new sign, their joint had become so well known that the name stuck. There are dozens of locations, but here's the address for the original. *1006 N. Highland Ave., Atlanta, GA 30306, 404-873-6529, www.tacomac.com*

LAST-MINUTE TIPS

Where to Shop: Atlantic Station is located close to the Georgia Tech campus between Sixteenth and Seventeenth streets. There are plenty of restaurants, pubs, stores, and a movie theater.

Where to Buy Tickets: Ticket City (www.ticketcity.com) is the official ticket broker of Georgia Tech athletics.

Marlow's Tavern: Marlow's is a neighborhood tavern with contemporary features. The décor combines brick walls with a modern black and white motif. The menu is varied with everything from burgers and tavern-sized sandwiches to entrees such as shrimp and grits. *950 West Peachtree St., Atlanta, GA 30309, 404-815-0323,* _www.marlowstavern.com_

Hudson Grille: The Hudson Grille bills itself as Atlanta's best sports bar and it's hard to argue. There are HD TVs everywhere, multiple bars, and enough space for large groups. There are several Hudson Grille locations. The Midtown bar is the closest to the Tech campus. *942 Peachtree Rd., Atlanta, GA 30309, 404-892-0892,* _www.hudsongrille.com_

TRAVELING TO ATLANTA?

Atlanta's Hartsfield International Airport is one of the busiest airports in the world. Delta offers direct flights from Syracuse to Atlanta. Likewise, there are multiple flight options from New York City and Washington, D.C. The drive time from Syracuse to Atlanta is a little under sixteen hours.

Louisville

On April 3, 1778, a group of eight prominent men in a two-decade-old settlement declared their intention to open the Jefferson Seminary. They started raising money and gaining support for the project.

The seminary opened in 1813, becoming the first city-owned public college in the United States. It closed in 1829 but was replaced by the Louisville Medical Institute, chartered in 1833 and opened in 1837. That same year, the rival Louisville Collegiate Institute was chartered. In 1840, LCI became the Louisville College. Four years later, LC took over the portion of the estate that was used for the Jefferson Seminary.

In 1846, the Kentucky State Legislature ordered Louisville College and the Louisville Medical Institute to consolidate with a new law school. The combination was called the University of Louisville. But it did not survive financially.

In 1907, it was revived as a liberal arts institution. The University of Louisville has since grown into a prestigious in-city institution. In 1970, the legislature made it part of the Kentucky public education system. Nowadays, under the direction of President James R. Ramsey, the University of Louisville focuses on the fields of teaching and research and stresses service to the community.

The Louisville Cardinals have a rich history in sports. The university ascended from independent status, from 1911 to 1925, to membership in the Kentucky Intercollegiate Athletic Conference (1925-1948), Ohio Valley Conference (1948-1949), independent again (1949-1964), Missouri Valley Conference (1964-1975), Metro Conference (1975-1995), Conference USA (1995-2005), to a Syracuse University rival in the Big East from 2005 to 2012. Louisville announced in November 2012, that it, too, was leaving the Big East for the ACC.

The Cardinals' national prominence in football and basketball attracted the ACC, which selected Louisville to replace Maryland. Also attractive, though, is the widespread Louisville sports success. The Cardinals have won eighteen regular-season and thirty-four conference tournament titles in their past conferences.

Some people might consider Louisville a basketball school. The Cardinals' men's basketball team has made the NCAA Final Four ten times, and Denny Crum coached them to a pair of national titles, in 1980 and 1986. Rick Pitino came from the NBA to take over for Crum in 2001. The former assistant to Jim Boeheim at SU has continued his college coaching success, which included a Final Four while leading Providence and a national title at Kentucky. He has guided Louisville to the Final Four three times, in 2005 and 2012, and won the 2013 national championship.

The Cardinals are a player on the football field, too. The pipe-smoking Howard Schnellenberger earned a breakout season at 10-1-1 in 1990. Great seasons also have come under John L. Smith, at 11-2 in 2001; Bobby Petrino, at 12-1 in 2006; and current coach Charlie Strong, at 11-2 with a BCS victory over Florida, last season.

PROGRAM HIGHLIGHTS

Football

NATIONAL CHAMPIONSHIPS (0): Louisville has appeared in two Bowl Championship Series games. After the 2006 season, the Cardinals beat Wake Forest 24-13 in the Orange Bowl, and topped Florida after last season in the Sugar Bowl.

BOWL RECORD: 8-8-1 (.500). Last bowl—33-23 over Florida in the 2013 Sugar Bowl

LONGEST WINNING STREAK: 11 games (twice), 2004-2005

WINNINGEST COACH: Frank Camp (1946-1968), 118-95-2, 54.8 percent

HEISMAN TROPHY WINNERS OR HIGHEST HEISMAN FINISH: Quarterback Brian Brohm, 2007, 10th place

Basketball

NATIONAL CHAMPIONSHIPS (4): NAIA: 1948; NCAA: 1980, 1986, 2013

ACC CHAMPIONSHIPS (0): The Cardinals will bring twenty-two regular-season and eighteen tournament titles with them to the ACC from time spent in the Kentucky Intercollegiate Athletic Conference, Metro Conference, Conference USA, and the Big East. Louisville won a share of the 2013 regular season crown and the title of the Big East Tournament, beating Syracuse 78-61 in the final.

NCAA TOURNAMENT RECORD: 70-40 (.636) Last NCAA appearance—An 82-76 win over Michigan in the 2013 championship game.

WINNINGEST COACH: Denny Crum (1971-2001), 675-295 (.696)

NATIONAL PLAYERS OF THE YEAR: Darrell Griffith (1980 Wooden Award)

LEGENDS

Wes Unseld

Wes Unseld decided to go to his hometown college in 1965. All of Louisville got to appreciate the mountain of a man. Unseld wasn't tall for a man in the middle, listed at 6-foot-7. He was, however, the guy they may have coined the phrase "wide body" for, listed at 245 pounds. On the Louisville freshman team, Unseld averaged an astounding 35.8 points and 23.6 rebounds a game. During his three varsity seasons, Louisville went 60-22 as Unseld averaged a double-double, at 20.6 points and 18.9 rebounds a game. The Cardinals went to the NIT in 1966 and the NCAA Tournament in 1967 and 1968, and Unseld was a consensus All-American his junior and senior seasons. He went on to more fame in the NBA with the Baltimore and then Washington Bullets. His rookie season, Unseld won both the Rookie of the Year and Most Valuable Player awards. He went on to be a five-time All-Star and led the Bullets to an NBA title in 1978. His No. 31 is retired by Louisville, and Unseld is in the Naismith Basketball Hall of Fame.

Darrell Griffith

Yes, Darrell Griffith could put on a dunking display. His ability to get up there and jam earned him the nickname of Dr. Dunkenstein. But the shooting guard was so much more than that during his four-year career at Louisville. Griffith left for the NBA in 1980 as the all-time Cardinals scoring leader, with 2,333 points. Louisville was 101-25 in his four years, capped by the biggest prize of all, the 1980 NCAA Tournament title. He scored in double figures his last 41 games as a Cardinal and notched 10 or more points in 111 of his 126 games at Louisville. Griffith won the Wooden Award for National Player of the Year for his senior season before going on to become the NBA Rookie of the Year in 1981. Griffith spent his entire eleven-year NBA career with the Utah Jazz.

Pervis Ellison

How cool was this center during his Louisville career? Ellison earned the nickname "Never Nervous Pervis" as he became the No. 2 all-time scorer in school history. As a freshman, he led the Cardinals to their NCAA title in 1986, and was the first freshman since 1944 to be named the most oustanding player in the Final Four. Ellison was the first Cardinal to score more than 2,000 points and pull down more than 1,000 rebounds in a career. After his consensus All-American status his senior year, Ellison was the first pick overall in the NBA draft, selected by the Sacramento Kings. Knee injuries slowed Ellison during his eleven-year NBA career.

Johnny Unitas

Louisville was 0-4 when Head Coach Frank Camp put freshman quarterback Johnny Unitas into a game in 1951. (Louisville wasn't a member of the NCAA back then, so the freshman-ineligible rule did not apply.) Unitas led the Cardinals from a 19-0 deficit to St. Bonaventure, completing eleven straight passes on the way to taking a 21-19 lead. The Bonnies kicked a last-minute field goal to win, but Unitas then led Louisville to four straight wins. He could throw during a run-happy era, completing 247 of 503 passes for 2,912 yards and 27 TDs. His No. 16 is the only football jersey retired by Louisville. Of course, Unitas went on to his legendary career with the Baltimore Colts wearing No. 19. But not before the Pittsburgh Steelers drafted Unitas in the ninth round and cut him. Two NFL championships and a Super Bowl title later, Unitas was still being cheered by Louisville fans.

Elvis Dumervil

The Miami native started to come on strong for Coach Bobby Petrino during his junior season, compiling ten sacks and eleven tackles for a loss. As a senior, he was the man. He set the NCAA record for sacks in a single game, racking up six against rival Kentucky. He went on to break the season sack record of Orangeman Dwight Freeney. Dumervil won the 2005 Big East Player of the Year Award, was a consensus All-American and won the Bronko Nagurski and Ted Hendricks trophies. Dumervil continued to be a sacks machine in the NFL after being drafted in the fourth round by the Denver Broncos, making the Pro Bowl three times and leading the league in sacks in 2009.

NOTABLE ALUMS

Sue Grafton
Author of popular detective novels

Donald Baxter
Discovered first safe intravenous fluid

James Patterson
Founder of Long John Silver's, Rally's Hamburgers, and Chi-Chi's restaurants

Delfeayo Marsalis
Jazz trombonist

ARENA

The KFC Yum! Center: The KFC Yum! Center had some big arena shoes to fill when it opened in 2010. The modern basketball palace fits 22,000 in downtown Louisville, on the banks of the Ohio River. The Cardinals have had success in its big-time atmosphere, with a winning percentage of nearly .900 in their first three seasons at Yum! The new arena replaced a home court that cast a large shadow. In Freedom Hall, on the grounds of the Kentucky Fair and Exposition, Louisville compiled a record of 664-136 over fifty-four seasons. Freedom Hall was big and famous. Just shy of 20,000 could fit. For Louisville's final game in Freedom, a record 20,135 squeezed in to watch the Cardinals beat top-ranked Syracuse.

STADIUM

Papa John's Cardinal Stadium: Papa John's Cardinal Stadium had room for 42,000 fans when it was built in 1998. It took Louisville officials just a decade to decide that wasn't enough red seats for Cardinals fans. A two-year expansion was finished in 2010, upping the capacity to 55,000. The on-campus facility has room to get even bigger. The latest reconfiguration left room for a plan to go up to 80,000 in the future. The Cardinals love the place. They won twenty straight home games between 2004 and 2007 before falling 38-35 to Syracuse.

CUSE CONNECTION

ALL-TIME FOOTBALL RECORD VS. SYRACUSE: 6-6

Last meeting November 10, 2012: Syracuse 45, Louisville 26

ALL-TIME BASKETBALL RECORD VS. SYRACUSE: 15-7

Last meeting March 16, 2013 (Big East Tournament championship game): Louisville 78, Syracuse 61

Coaching rivals: The career paths of Jim Boeheim and Rick Pitino entangled in 1976, just two years after Pitino was a point guard at Providence. His first coaching job was an assistant at Hawaii. His second was on Boeheim's bench in Syracuse from 1976 to 1978. Their teams have clashed fiercely since. In 1987, Boeheim led Syracuse to a 77-63 victory over Pitino's Providence squad in the Final Four. In 1996, Pitino led Kentucky to a 76-67 win over Syracuse in the the NCAA championship game. Since Pitino took over at Louisville, his teams hold a 8-4 mark over Boeheim's Orange. They've been known to verbally jab, too. After it was announced that Syracuse and Pittsburgh were leaving the Big East for the ACC, Pitino declared that Memphis and Temple would be more than suitable replacements. At a subsequent Big East media day, Boeheim and Pitino each said the other was full of it. Louisville is joining the ACC, too. May the sideline passion continue.

For none of the marbles: Coach Roy Danforth led SU to the Final Four in 1975, winning the ECAC championship along the way, and then beating La Salle, North Carolina, and Kansas State in the NCAA Tournament. Alas, the Final Four was in San Diego, but it was the Bluegrass State that would deflate Syracuse's high hopes. The Orange fell 95-79 in the semifinals. In the consolation game, Denny Crum's Cardinals won in overtime, 96-88. In a season in which Rudy Hackett led the Orange in scoring—22.2 points per game—and rebounding—12.7 per game—Syracuse ended up 23-9. Louisville, which had lost 75-74 in overtime to UCLA in the semifinals, finished the season 28-3.

The last at Freedom Hall: Syracuse won thirty games and lost just five in the 2009-10 season. And the Orange was 0-2 vs. Louisville. Syracuse was ranked second in the nation when the two tangled on February 14, 2010, but the Cardinals left the Carrier Dome on top 66-60. Three weeks later, Syracuse was No. 1 when it visited Louisville, and this time the Cardinals prevailed 78-68. In that second matchup, Scoop Jardine had twenty points and Wes Johnson eighteen for the Orange, but all they could do was watch as Louisville fans stormed the court because the Cardinals won their last game ever in Freedom Hall.

MASCOT

The Cardinal was first adopted as Louisville's mascot in 1913 to honor the Kentucky state bird. The teams' vivid Cardinal red uniforms didn't come until later. The Cardinal Bird is the official name of the costumed creature that's been known to skydive into Papa John's Cardinal Stadium to inspire home football crowds. The mascot has become known as "Louie" in some circles, or even C.B. for short.

OTHER SPORTS

Big East fans know about Louisville's league success in basketball and football, what with that Final Four appearance and BCS bowl victory both coming at the end of the 2012 seasons. But the Cardinals have found success this century in other sports, too. Since 2000, the women's basketball team has reached the NCAA Final Four twice, the baseball team has made it to the College World Series, and the men's soccer team has advanced to the College Cup National Title Game. That's a lot of tradition of success the Cardinals will be bringing across the fields and courts of the ACC.

GAME DAY

MEDIA

Broadcasting the Game: WHAS-AM 840 and WKRD-AM 740/FM 101.7 in Louisville, WCKY-AM 1530 in Cincinnati

Covering the Cardinals: www.courier-journal.com (*Louisville Courier-Journal*), www.louisvillecardinal.com (Louisville student newspaper), espn.go.com/blog/bigeast (ESPN Big East blog)

TAILGATING

Tailgating is allowed, with several caveats. No throwing of footballs or anything else in the Papa John's Cardinal Stadium lots. All beverages must be poured into a plastic cup and consumed near your car. The stadium lots open five hours before game time. Street festival booths will open three hours before game time. And the stadium entrances open two hours before game time. Papa John's Cardinal Stadium lots are mostly filled by contributors and season ticket holders with lot passes. Visitors are encouraged to park at the Kentucky Fair and Exposition Center lots, which are expansive. Admission to the lot is $8, and it is walking distance to the stadium. The same tailgating rules apply.

The KFC Yum! Center, meanwhile, has a parking garage. Its site says 22,000 spots are available to basketball fans in the surrounding blocks. For information go to www.kfcyumcenter.com/plan-your-visit/directions-parking. For information, go to www.pjcardinalstadium.com.

SHUTTLE

There is a shuttle for handicapped football game patrons from the Floyd Street garage. For information go to louisville.edu/athletics/papajohns/venueinfo.htm#Ticket%20Exchange.

TRADITIONS

Card March: Fans flock to the lot outside Papa John's Cardinal Stadium to wish Coach Charlie Strong and his men well. The Cardinal Marching Band leads the way as team members walk from the bus to the stadium.

Victory Lap: Coach John L. Smith had his players start a tradition to make sure the fans know how much they appreciate the U of L spirit. After each game, the Cardinals won't leave the field without first completing a victory lap. It's not quite a Lambeau Leap, but they get up close and personal to slap high-fives and share the moment with fans who love to press close.

ABOUT TOWN

In 1778, George Rogers Clark settled into the area on the banks of the Ohio River and named it after King Louis XVI of France. In the nineteenth century, Louisville's location made it an important internal shipping port. Now, its metropolitan population of 1.3 million ranks Louisville as the biggest city in Kentucky and the forty-second-biggest metro area in the country. The metropolitan area includes counties in northern Kentucky and southern Indiana. Louisville is sometimes called the northernmost city of the South and sometimes called the southernmost city of the north. In any case, sporting eyes turn to Louisville's Churchill Downs each May for the running of the Kentucky Derby, the first of thoroughbred horse racing's heralded Triple Crown.

LODGING

Marriott Downtown: For those who want to be in the bustling city and close to the KFC Yum! Center, the Marriott fits the bill. It's connected to the Convention Center and one block from the arena. It also has three restaurants on site: the BLU Italian Grille, Champions, and a Starbucks. *280 W. Jefferson St., Louisville, KY 40202, 502-627-5045, www.marriott.com/hotels/travel/sdflm-louisville-marriott-downtown*

Hilton Garden Inn: This edition of the popular Hilton brand is close to the airport. It's also next to the Kentucky Fair and Exposition Center and close to Papa John's Cardinal Stadium. Call that location, location, location. It features the Great American Grill. *2735 Crittenden Dr., Louisville, KY 40209, 502-637-2424, hilton-gardeninn3.hilton.com/en/hotels/kentucky/hilton-garden-inn-louisville-airport*

Residence Inn: The downtown location of Marriott's family- and pet-friendly brand has been newly renovated. All guests are invited to chow down on the free breakfast. Don't worry. You can work it off in the 24-hour fitness center and pool or walk it off downtown. *330 E. Main St., Louisville, KY 40202, 502-589-8998, www.marriott.com/hotels/travel/sdfgj-residence-inn-louisville-downtown*

EATING

Cardinal Hall of Fame Cafe: The perfect spot for college sports fans to eat, drink, and be merry about University of Louisville heroes, the cafe is part museum, with a Walk of Fame. Cabinets hold memorabilia donated by U of L athletes and fans. Tiles on the floor are laid in order of induction, each in honor of an athlete or coach who is in the Cardinal Hall of Fame. The menu features burgers, pasta, seafood, and pizza. *2745 Crittenden Dr., Louisville, KY 40209, 502-635-8686, www.halloffamecafes.com/prod/cardinal*

Impellizzeri's Pizza: Benny Impellizzeri began making pizzas at night because the butcher's shop his father bought to run by day came equipped with ovens. In 1979, Impellizzeri's Pizza was born. Benny made his pies with two layers of toppings and two layers of cheese. To this day, that's now known as Louisville-style pizza. Impellizzeri's has grown to three locations, with the downtown place minutes from the KFC Yum! Center. *110 W. Main St., Louisville, KY 40202, 502-589-4900, www.impellizzeris.com*

Wick's Pizza Parlor and Pub: Michael Wickliffe opened the first Wick's in 1991. By serving pasta, Sandwicks, and a pizza called the Big Wick to fit the culinary and budget needs of students, sports fans, and, well, anybody in Louisville with a hankering for good food and beverages, Wick's has grown to five locations. The original sits amid coffee shops and other cool joints. *975 Baxter Ave., Louisville, KY 40204, 502-458-1828, www.wickspizza.com*

SIGHTSEEING

Churchill Downs: Louisville is home to arguably the most famous horse track in the world. The spires of Churchill Downs are unmistakable. Yes, it's home to the Kentucky Derby in May. There are, though, other races during other months, starting with an April session and extending through a fall finish that includes football season. *700 Central Ave., Louisville, KY 40215, 502-636-4400, www.churchilldowns.com*

Louisville Slugger Museum: Sure enough, the famous Louisville Slugger baseball bat is made in downtown Louisville. The museum and factory combines exhibits that commemorate the great wooden bat and the machines that still make it. Tour guides escort visitors through the grounds. And everybody who takes the tour gets handed a miniature wooden bat to mark the occasion. *800 W. Main St., Louisville, KY 40202, 877-775-8447, www.sluggermuseum.com*

SHOPPING

Mall St. Matthew's: Louisville's first true indoor mall was the Mall St. Matthew's. With more than 130 stores—that is, a brand for everyone—it's still considered one of the city's most popular shopping spots. *5000 Shelbyville Rd., Louisville, KY 40207, 502-893-0311, www.mallstmatthews.com*

Diva's Handbags and Accessories: The woman on the trip will want to check out the unique styles available in the store voted Louisville's best gift shop. And if it's just the man on the trip, the owner promises helpful clerks who can guide you to the right gift to bring home. *2429 Lime Kiln Lane, Louisville, KY 40222, 502-426-3355*

NIGHTLIFE

Molly Malone's Irish Pub: Molly Malone's features pub food. It's the Louisville home to Irish music. And, it was built from stones taken from a pub in Ireland. Now that's a foundation for fun, at either location, downtown or by the Mall St. Matthew's (which features more DJ-type music instead of the Irish sounds). *933 Baxter Ave., Louisville, KY 40204, 502-433-1222, www.mollymalonesirishpub.com*

Drake's: This joint was named by Brian McCarty and named after Bruce Drake. The website proudly says the neighborhood-style joint is "freewheeling and fun-loving," just like those two guys. The restaurant portion is known for great beer, and the bar portion is known for great food. That is a twist to brag about. *3939 Shelbyville Rd., Louisville, KY 40207, 502-614-7327, www.drakescomeplay.com*

O'Shea's: It all started with Mary O'Shea, who was born in Ireland and moved to Chicago at age nineteen. Mary landed in Louisville, where in 1958 she opened Mary's Chateau, known for its great atmosphere and live cabaret-style music. In the 1980s, the name changed to O'Shea's Irish Pub, and the focus expanded from music and drink to add pub food. *956 Baxter Ave., Louisville, KY 40204, 502-589-7373, www.osheaslouisville.net*

LAST-MINUTE TIPS

Where to Shop: Louisville is a big city, with plenty of shops of all sizes, shapes, and varieties happy to have you fork over the green or plastic so you can take what they're selling home. But on game day, there's no need to find that great T-shirt and souvenir joint elsewhere. Cardinal Authentic is located outside Gate 2 of Papa John's Cardinal Stadium. shop.uoflsports.com

Where to Buy Tickets: A walk through the parking lots of the Fair and Expo Center or stadium may allow you to connect with somebody looking to part with an extra ducat. Online, secondary sales sites stubhub.com and vividseats.com both sport clicks for Louisville football and basketball games.

TRAVELING TO LOUISVILLE?

The Louisville campus is only a seven-minute drive from Louisville International Airport. It's a nine-hour drive west from Washington, D.C., and ten and a half hours from Syracuse.

Miami

The University of Miami was formed in 1925 in Coral Gables, Florida—just south of Miami—as a non-sectarian, private university. It has grown over the last eighty-eight years to include twelve colleges, a medical school, law school, and school of oceanography and atmospheric science.

The University of Miami—or, simply, "The U," as it has come to be known from a football program that has regularly sent players on to become NFL stars—has a Syracuse connection at the very top. Donna Shalala, university president since 2001, received a doctorate at Syracuse University's Maxwell School of Citizenship and Public Affairs before becoming Secretary of Health and Human Services under President Bill Clinton.

The campus houses an extensive library that, true to its south Florida demographic and heritage, includes a large collection of holdings of Cuban heritage and music.

In 2012, *U.S. News and World Report* ranked the University of Miami No. 44 on its list of best colleges, the fourth straight year it was rated in the top 50.

UNIVERSITY OF MIAMI

STUDENTS
15,613

CORAL GABLES
pop. 47,783

SUN LIFE STADIUM
76,500

BANKUNITED CENTER
7,972

COLORS
Orange, Green, & White

NICKNAME
Hurricanes

MASCOT
Sebastian the Ibis

CAMPUS ATTRACTIONS
Jerry Herman Ring Theatre, John C. Gifford Arboretum and Botanical Gardens, Lowe Art Museum

PHONE
305-284-2211
(general information)

305-284-4443
(campus police)

305-284-3243
(athletic department)

TICKETS
305-284-2263 or
www.hurricanesports.com

The Hurricanes are notorious for their football program. The glory years include five national championships, spanning the period between 1983 and 2001. Four different coaches led Miami to the top: pipe-smoking, suit-wearing Howard Schnellenberger earned the first crown; Jimmy Johnson and Dennis Erickson foreshadowed their NFL fame, Johnson with a title in 1987 and Erickson snaring a pair, in 1989 and 1991; and Mighty Mouse assistant Larry Coker won it in 2001.

Miami football has had its share of scandals and reprimands, too. There was the alleged "pay for play" years in the 1980s, reportedly fueled by 2 Live Crew hip-hopper Luther Campbell; the Pell Grant controversy under Butch Davis in 1995; and the Nevin Shapiro illegal benefits exposé that led to self-imposed sanctions in 2010. Again, controversy swirled around the Shapiro incident when the NCAA admitted later that investigators had acted improperly.

Current coach Al Golden came from Temple University, and the Hurricanes were 6-6 in his first year and 7-5 this past season. The Hurricanes were bitter rivals with the Syracuse Orange in the Big East Conference between 1991 and 2003. Miami joined the ACC in 2004.

The Hurricanes basketball program has been less successful, until recently.

Yes, NBA Hall of Famer Rick Barry was a Hurricane in the 1960s. But the college actually dropped the sport in 1971, and didn't bring it back until 1985.

Bill Foster coached the 'Canes to a mark of 78-71 until 1990. Leonard Hamilton went 144-147 from 1990 to 2000 and took the Hurricanes to the NCAA Sweet Sixteen before leaving for the NBA's Washington Wizards and Michael Jordan. Perry Clark and Frank Haith both cracked the .500 mark, Clark at 65-54 and then Haith at 129-101 before leaving to take the job at Missouri in 2011. After Haith's departure, the NCAA started investigating improprieties during his Hurricanes tenure. Miami hired Jim Larranaga from George Mason University, where he coached the Patriots to the Final Four in 2006.

Larranaga's team went 20-13 in 2011-12. That was just a sign of things to come. In 2012-13, Miami became the first team to win its first ten ACC games since North Carolina in the 1980s and then captured the ACC regular-season and tournament titles.

PROGRAM HIGHLIGHTS

Football

NATIONAL CHAMPIONSHIPS (5): 1983, 1987, 1989, 1991, 2001

ACC CHAMPIONSHIPS (0): Miami has not won the Coastal Division title since joining the ACC in 2004. The Hurricanes have played in six bowl games as an ACC member, going 2-4.

BIG EAST CHAMPIONSHIPS (9): 1991, 1992, 1994, 1995, 1996, 2000, 2001, 2002, 2003

BOWL RECORD: 18-16 (.529). Last bowl—33-17 loss to Notre Dame in 2010 Sun Bowl. Miami voluntarily sat out bowls in 2011 and 2012 amid NCAA investigation.

LONGEST WINNING STREAK: 34 games, 2000-03, sixth longest of all-time

WINNINGEST COACH: Andy Gustafson (1948-1963), 93-65 (.587)

HEISMAN TROPHY WINNERS (2): Quarterback Vinny Testaverde (1986), quarterback Gino Torretta (1990)

Basketball

NATIONAL CHAMPIONSHIPS (0): The Hurricanes reached the NCAA Tournament Sweet Sixteen under Leonard Hamilton in 2000.

ACC CHAMPIONSHIPS (2): Regular season: (1) 2013; ACC Tournament (1) 2013

NCAA TOURNAMENT RECORD: 6-7 (.461) Last appearance—Lost 71-61 to Marquette in the 2013 Sweet 16

WINNINGEST COACH: Bruce Hale (1954-1967), 220-112 (.633)

CONSENSUS ALL-AMERICAN: Rick Barry (1965)

LEGENDS

Rick Barry
Barry came from New Jersey to star for the Hurricanes under Coach Bruce Hale. The small forward led the nation in scoring in his senior season, averaging 37.4 points. He was a 1965 consensus All-American. Known for his dead-eye outside shot and precise underhanded style from the free-throw line, Barry is one of just two Hurricanes to have his jersey retired. He went on to great things in the pros, becoming an NBA All-Star with the San Francisco Warriors and then becoming one of the first true stars to jump to the competing ABA.

Ted Hendricks
Playing defensive end for the Hurricanes from 1966 to 1968, Hendricks was credited with 327 tackles, the most ever for a Miami defensive lineman. His tall and relatively thin frame and energetic ways earned him the nickname "The Mad Stork." During a productive NFL career that included a Super Bowl title with the Baltimore Colts, the team that drafted him in the second round, and three more with the Oakland Raiders, his nickname was shortened to simply, "The Stork."

Jim Kelly
Before the four-straight Super Bowl appearances with the Buffalo Bills, Kelly directed the Hurricanes. The quarterback went south to Miami instead of his home state Penn State because Joe Paterno wanted him to play linebacker. Instead, Kelly started the Hurricanes QB dynasty that extended to Bernie Kosar, Vinny Testaverde, and Gino Torretta. Kelly threw for more than 5,000 yards and 32 touchdowns at Miami before signing with the USFL's Houston Gamblers in 1984.

Vinny Testaverde
Quarterback Testaverde almost had it all his senior season, winning the Heisman Trophy in 1986 as well as becoming a consensus All-American. He set the all-time Miami touchdown pass record with forty-seven. But in his final game before becoming a longtime pro, Testaverde threw for five interceptions as the favored Hurricanes lost to Penn State 14-10 in

the 1987 Fiesta Bowl, and the national championship was not to be. Testaverde lasted an astounding twenty years in the NFL, including two Pro Bowl seasons, one with the Baltimore Ravens and one with the New York Jets.

Russell Maryland

Miami was the only major college to offer Maryland a scholarship out of high school. Oh, how the defensive tackle rewarded the Hurricanes. In his four seasons, Maryland recorded 279 tackles, including 25 for a loss of yards and 20.5 sacks. In 1990, he became the first Hurricane to win the Outland Trophy, given to the best lineman in the country. During his Miami career, the Hurricanes did not lose at home, went to four bowl games, and won two national titles. In the NFL, Maryland was productive for a decade with the Cowboys, Raiders, and Packers.

NOTABLE ALUMS

Dwayne "The Rock" Johnson
Pro wrestler and actor

Ray Liotta
Actor, *Goodfellas* and *Field of Dreams*

Sylvester Stallone
Actor and all things *Rocky*

Donald Justice
1980 Pulitzer Prize winner for poetry

Gloria Estefan
Five-time Grammy winner

Grace Slick
Jefferson Airplane singer

Dan Le Batard
Miami Herald columnist and ESPN host

ARENA

BankUnited Center: The BankUnited Center is a multi-purpose, on-campus arena. It opened in 2003 as the University of Miami Convocation Center. In addition to Hurricanes men's and women's basketball, it hosts concerts and other sporting events, such as boxing. In 2004, it hosted the first presidential debate between President George W. Bush and challenger John Kerry.

STADIUM

Sun Life Stadium: The expansive Sun Life Stadium opened in 1987, essentially replacing the venerable Orange Bowl. Talk about big shoes to fill. It opened as Joe Robbie Stadium, named after the Miami Dolphins owner who spearheaded the private financing for its construction. It was the first stadium to include a club level with executive seating. It has hosted five Super Bowls, two World Series, and four college football national championship games. The Orange Bowl game itself moved to the new stadium in 1996; the Hurricanes moved there in 2008, the year the Orange Bowl Stadium was demolished. Marlins Park now stands at the site.

CUSE CONNECTION

Last meeting November 15, 2003: Miami 17, Syracuse 10

Last meeting February 14, 2004: Syracuse 91, Miami 74

Gedney stopped short: On November 21, 1992, the Carrier Dome was roaring as Syracuse quarterback Marvin Graves was leading the Orange up the field for a possible winning touchdown against the undefeated Hurricanes. Graves found Central New York's favorite son Chris Gedney for a twenty-nine-yard completion as the clock ran out. Alas, Miami's Casey Greer shoulder-tackled the tight end from Liverpool High School on the three-yard line. It was the final game of the regular season for Syracuse, which beat Colorado in the Fiesta Bowl to finish 10-2 and ranked No. 6. Miami extended its winning streak to twenty-nine games in its season finale vs. San Diego State, but fell to Alabama in the Sugar Bowl and finished 11-1 and No. 2.

Glorious dome finale for McNabb: Star Syracuse quarterback Donovan McNabb saved something very special for his last game at the Carrier Dome as the senior led the Orange to an astonishing 66-13 demolition of the Hurricanes on November 28, 1998. It was Miami's worst loss since 1944. The win gave the Orange a regular-season record of 8-3 and Syracuse's third straight Big East title. Alas, Syracuse lost to Florida 31-0 in the Orange Bowl.

Hello Miami: The first time the Orange met the Hurricanes in basketball was on December 28, 1963, in Miami. It was a notable game because it went into overtime, future Hall of Famer Dave Bing led Syracuse with twenty-nine points, and the two schools would not meet on the basketball court again for twenty-nine years.

Defense fit for a king: It might have seemed like a run-of-the-mill, end-of-January game in 2003 as Syracuse traveled to Coral Gables to beat Miami 54-49. But to close the game, Syracuse showed defense designed for really big things, holding Miami scoreless for the last 8:38 of the game to secure the victory. Hakim Warrick led Syracuse with eighteen points and three blocked shots. Remember him as the lanky guy who blocked the last-second Kansas shot a couple of months later to secure Syracuse's lone national championship.

MASCOT

In 1926, the Ibis became the name of the Miami yearbook and its unofficial mascot. It was chosen for the marsh bird that is noted for bravery in the face of hurricanes. Yet a bulldog named Hurricane I was the official mascot on the sidelines until 1957. That's when Sebastian the Ibus was born as a homecoming contest entry, a costumed mascot named after the campus's popular San Sebastián dorm.

OTHER SPORTS

Plenty of folks in Coral Gables would bristle at the thought of the baseball program being considered in the "other sports" category. Here's how good the Hurricanes are on the diamond: forty straight NCAA Tournament regional appearances; twenty-three College World Series appearances; four national championships. The Hurricanes play at Mark Light Field at Alex Rodriguez Stadium. Yup, A-Rod was a Hurricane before that big career with Seattle, Texas, and the Yankees.

GAME DAY

MEDIA

Broadcasting the Game: WQAM 560 AM in Miami; WVUM 90.5 FM in Coral Gables; Radio Coracol 1260 AM (Spanish, football)

Covering the Hurricanes: www.miamiherald.com (*Miami Herald*), www.themiamihurricane.com (UM student newspaper), espn.go.com/blog/playbook/fandom (ESPN Miami blog)

TAILGATING

Tailgating is allowed, but only one spot can be taken per vehicle. Barbecues are allowed, but no grills in tow. No beer kegs. Gates open four hours before game time. Fee is $25 per car. For information go to www.sunlifestadium.com/parking.

There are two parking lots outside of BankUnited Center for basketball games. The arena is located across the street from the University Metrorail Station. For information, go to www.bankunitedcenter.com/directions_parking.

SHUTTLE

There is no shuttle service for football games.

TRADITIONS

Hurricane Walk: Early arrivers can take part in one of Miami's newest traditions, the Hurricane Walk. Fans form a human chain between Sun Life Stadium gates H to A. Two hours before game time, the players walk through the chain to the stadium, accompanied by the pomp of the marching band, named the Band of the Hour, and spirit squad.

Run Through the Smoke: Right before game time, another grand entrance awaits the Hurricanes as they take the field. Billowing white smoke unfurls from a series of pipes. (If you must look behind the green curtain, it's fire extinguisher exhaust.) The much-copied tradition started at Miami in the 1950s.

ABOUT TOWN

Coral Gables was one of America's first planned communities, developed by George Thomas Merrick in the Florida land boom of the 1920s. It's known as a walking-friendly community of such striking appearance that it bills itself as The City Beautiful . . . with the website to back it up, www.citybeautiful.net. The city has a population of about 47,000. Of course, since it sits in Miami-Dade County, just south of Miami Beach, it offers a culturally diverse world to visitors.

DRIVE, DRIVE YOU HURRICANES

LODGING

The Biltmore Hotel: When the Biltmore Hotel was built in 1926, it was the tallest building in Florida. It's lived an interesting life since. During World War II, the Biltmore was converted into a hospital. After that, it was a Veterans Administration Hospital, then a campus facility for the U of M's Medical School. It reopened as a hotel in 1987. It's often used as a location for film and TV shoots. The Biltmore sits on 150 natural acres and is surrounded by a Donald Ross–designed golf course. On Sundays, guests are offered a free walking tour of the grounds. *1200 Anastasia Ave., Coral Gables, FL 33134, 855-311-6903, www.biltmorehotel.com*

Westin Colonnade: This edition of the Westin chain sits in the heart of the Coral Gables stretch of the bustling district known as the Miracle Mile. Its hospitality includes the amenities it calls its Heavenly Bed and Heavenly Bath. *180 Aragon Ave., Coral Gables, FL 33134, 305-441-2600, www. westincoralgables.com*

EATING

Palme d'or: Located in the historic Biltmore Hotel (described above), the Palme d'or features haute French cuisine from the mind and heart of Chef Philippe Ruiz. The Palme d'or was selected as the best restaurant in Coral Gables by the *Miami New Times*. It features a seasonally changing menu. *1200 Anastasia Ave., Coral Gables, FL 33134, 305-913-3201, www.biltmorehotel.com*

Caffe Abbracci: Since 1988, host Nino Pernitti has offered the Old World elegance of his beloved Venice. The time-tested recipes explore Italian style from antipasti to pastas. *318 Aragon Ave., Coral Gables, FL 33134, caffeabbracci.com*

News Cafe: Veteran Syracuse sports reporter Donnie Webb calls this one his don't-miss spot. Located on a busy corner in South Beach, the News Cafe started in 1988 as a quaint newspaper/magazine kiosk with tables sprinkled around it. Music offerings range from jazz to classical. The menu is simple American traditional. The idea is to sit, watch, listen, eat, enjoy. *800 Ocean Dr., Miami Beach, FL 33139, 305-538-6397*

SIGHTSEEING

Merrick House and Gardens: George E. Merrick founded Coral Gables. His historic home has been restored to its 1920s splendor since the city acquired it in 1976. It's on the U.S. National Register of Historic Places. Tours are held twice a week. Enjoy a spot on the breezy veranda. *997 Coral Way, Coral Gables, FL 33134, 305-460-5361, www.coralgables.com*

Venetian Pool: Part water park, part historic site, the Venetian Pool is billed as the world's most glamorous municipal pool. The pool was constructed in 1923 from a coral rock quarry. The grounds include two towers that overlook Coral Gables. It's a spot for both swimming and sunbathing. *2701 De Soto Blvd., Coral Gables, FL 33134, 305-460-5356, www.coralgables.com*

Fairchild Tropical Botanical Gardens: Fairchild is the largest tropical botanical gardens in the world. A tram ride takes visitors through eighty-three acres full of lush plants and exotic birds. *10901 Old Cutler Rd., Coral Gables, FL 33156, 305-667-1651, www.fairchildgarden.org*

North and South Beaches: South Beach gets the publicity for its throbbing nightlife, but don't forget that visitors can explore North Beach and its cool neighborhoods of Biscayne Point, Isle of Normandy, and La Gorce, too.

SHOPPING

Miracle Mile: When George E. Merrick designed Coral Gables, he liked to brag that everything was located within a two-block walk. Ninety years later, that stretch is called the Miracle Mile. It runs between Douglas and Le Jeune roads and West 37th and West 42nd streets. It's home to restaurants, bars, and plenty of specialty shops. www.shopcoralgables.com

Aventura Mall: A journey down Biscayne Boulevard will take visitors to Aventura Mall. It's full of luxury boutiques, fine dining, and a pretty spiffy food court. *19501 Biscayne Blvd., Aventura, FL 33180, 305-935-1110, www.aventuramall.com*

Coconut Grove: If you want to take a step away from hustle and bustle, Coconut Grove is the shopping spot for you. It's a waterfront community that sits between Biscayne Bay and U.S. Route 1. It's motto: "Always cool . . . Always hot." www.coconutgrove.com

NIGHTLIFE

The Bar: In the early evening, The Bar looks and feels like a cool English Pub, complete with dark wood and plenty of thick and tasty beer. Later, the dance floor gets full, the music gets loud, and The Bar caters to more exotic tastes. So much so that it's considered a top tequila spot. *172 Giralda Ave., Coral Gables, FL 33134, 305-442-2730,* www.gablesthebar.com

Titanic Brewery: The Titanic Brewery caters to lovers of carefully crafted beers in a big way. In fact, patrons can watch the beers get turned out behind the bar as they sit and savor. The Sampler offers brew lovers a choice of six of the nine microbrews made at the Titanic. It's a seafood restaurant, too. *5813 Ponce de Leon Blvd., Coral Gables, FL 33146, 305-668-1742,* www. titanicbrewery.com

---

LAST-MINUTE TIPS

Where to Shop: Downtown Coral Gables features a stretch of shopping called the Miracle Mile. Put on your best walking shoes and get to it.

Where to Buy Tickets: Demand seldom meets supply at the massive Sun Life Stadium. If you can't secure tickets through the university site, stubhub.com could work for you.

The Rathskeller: Go ahead, rub elbows with the fraternity brothers and sorority sisters of the U. The Rathskeller was founded in 1972 as a campus gathering spot for students, faculty, and staff. Visitors can grab a burger, quaff a beer, and be entertained by student bands, poetry slams, dance contests, and the Friday Night Belly Bust, featuring standup comics. *1306 Stanford Dr., Coral Gables, FL 33146, 305-284-6310, www.urathskeller.com*

TRAVELING TO CORAL GABLES?

Coral Gables is served by two major airports. The closest is Miami International, seven miles from campus. That can be a good choice during basketball season. Fort Lauderdale International is thirty-one miles away. That's a preferred landing spot during football season because it's closer to Sun Life Stadium than Miami. Want to drive from Syracuse? The trip is 1,415 miles due south, listed as 20 hours, 52 minutes (if you take shifts and don't stop to sleep).

North Carolina

In December of 1789, the North Carolina General Assembly chartered a bill calling for the establishment of a state university. Two years later, according to legend, William Davie, a Revolutionary War general and a member of the North Carolina General Assembly, rode out on his horse to find a location for the university. He stopped under a poplar tree near the town of Chapel Hill, and after enjoying a pleasant lunch Davie decided that the tree marked the perfect spot for the state university.

Alas, the story of Davie and the poplar tree are just legend. The site of the university was actually determined by a six-member committee. However, Davie did oversee the ceremonial setting of the cornerstone of the university's first building in 1793. That building, known as Old East, remains in use as a residence hall.

While the story behind it may be a tall tale, the Davie Poplar, now over 350 years old, still stands on the northern edge of the University of North Carolina. It's said that young lovers who kiss on the bench located under the Davie Poplar are destined to be married.

UNIVERSITY OF NORTH CAROLINA

STUDENTS
17,895

CHAPEL HILL
pop. 57,233

KENAN STADIUM
63,000

DEAN E. SMITH CENTER
21,750

COLORS
Carolina Blue & White

NICKNAME
Tar Heels

MASCOT
Rameses

CAMPUS ATTRACTIONS
Old Well, Silent Sam, Morehead Bell Tower

PHONE
919-962-5106
(general information)

919-962-3951
(campus police)

919-962-8200
(athletic department)

TICKETS
919-962-2296 or
www.goheels.com

Davie later became a member of the university's board of trustees. He served as North Carolina's governor. In 1811, the university awarded Davie with its first honorary degree and bestowed upon him the title "Father of the University."

The University of North Carolina opened its classroom doors in 1795, making it one of the nation's first public universities. The University of North Carolina thrived during the 1800s. In 1831, UNC became the first state university with an astronomical observatory. The university remained open during the Civil War, one of the few universities in the Confederacy to do so. However, the university shut down during Reconstruction from 1870 to 1875 due to a lack of funding.

Shortly after reopening its doors, the university fielded its first football team in 1888. In its first official game, North Carolina lost to Wake Forest.

In 1922, North Carolina joined the Southern Conference and won the conference title that fall with a 9-1 overall record and a 5-0 mark in the league. The Tar Heels enjoyed a huge amount of success when Charlie "Choo-Choo" Justice arrived in 1946. He led UNC to the Sugar Bowl in both 1947 and 1949 and the Cotton Bowl in 1950. North Carolina remained a member of the Southern Conference until joining the Atlantic Coast Conference in 1953. North Carolina has produced numerous All-Americans and sent dozens of players to the NFL, including Lawrence Taylor, Dre Bly, and Julius Peppers.

Many fans of North Carolina basketball instantly recall Dean Smith, Phil Ford, and Michael Jordan, but the Tar Heels were very good long before Smith first held up four fingers to signal his famous Four Corners offense.

North Carolina played its first game on January 27, 1911, defeating Virginia Christian. In 1924, the Tar Heels went 24-0, won the Southern Conference, and were later proclaimed national champions by the Helms Foundation. In 1952, Frank McGuire became the Tar Heels' head coach. One year later, North Carolina joined the ACC. In 1957, All-American Lennie Rosenbluth led the Tar Heels to a perfect 32-0 season. In the NCAA Tournament championship game, the Tar Heels defeated Kansas and its All-American Wilt Chamberlain, 54-53, in three overtimes.

McGuire left UNC after the 1960-61 season. The university promoted McGuire's assistant, Dean Smith, to the head coaching chair. The Tar Heels went 35-27 in Smith's first three seasons. Some fans called for Smith to be fired. Three years later, Smith led North Carolina to the 1967 Final Four. The year after that, the Tar Heels lost to UCLA in the championship game.

PROGRAM HIGHLIGHTS

Football

NATIONAL CHAMPIONSHIPS (0)

ACC CHAMPIONSHIPS (5): 1963, 1971, 1972, 1977, 1980

BOWL RECORD: 13-15 (.464). Last bowl—30-27 over Tennessee in 2010 Music City Bowl

LONGEST WINNING STREAK: 14 games, 1898-99

WINNINGEST COACH: Dick Crum (1978-87), 72-41-3 (.637)

HEISMAN TROPHY WINNERS OR HIGHEST HEISMAN FINISH: Running back Charlie Justice, 1948 and 1949 runner-up

Basketball

NATIONAL CHAMPIONSHIPS (5): 1957, 1982, 1993, 2005, 2009

ACC REGULAR SEASON CHAMPIONSHIPS (30): 1946, 1956, 1957, 1959, 1960, 1961, 1967, 1968, 1969, 1971, 1972, 1976, 1977, 1978, 1979, 1982, 1983, 1984, 1985, 1987, 1988, 1993, 1995, 2001, 2005, 2007, 2008, 2009, 2011, 2012

ACC TOURNAMENT CHAMPIONSHIPS (17): 1957, 1967, 1968, 1969, 1972, 1975, 1977, 1979, 1981, 1982, 1989, 1991, 1994, 1997, 1998, 2007, 2008

NCAA TOURNAMENT RECORD: 109-42 (.721) Last appearance—A 70-58 loss to Kansas in the second round of the 2013 tournament.

WINNINGEST COACH: Dean Smith (1962-1997), 879-254 (.776)

NATIONAL PLAYERS OF THE YEAR: Phil Ford (1978), Michael Jordan (1984), Antawn Jamison (1998), and Tyler Hansbrough (2008)

In thirty-six seasons, Smith would coach North Carolina to eleven Final Fours and two national titles. His teams won thirteen ACC tournaments. He retired in 1997 with 879 career victories, the most of any college coach at the time.

Smith's longtime assistant Bill Guthridge had the unenviable task of following Smith. Matt Doherty, a former Tar Heels player and a starter on the 1982 NCAA championship team, was the head coach for three years until

North Carolina hired Kansas head coach Roy Williams, a UNC alum who had been an assistant under Smith, in 2003.

Williams led North Carolina to NCAA titles in 2005 and 2009. In 2007, Williams was inducted into the Naismith Memorial Basketball Hall of Fame in Springfield, Massachusets, joining eight former Tar Heel players and coaches, including Dean Smith, Michael Jordan, and James Worthy.

LEGENDS

Lawrence Taylor
Regarded as the best outside linebacker in NFL history, Taylor had made a name for himself long before his pro career with the New York Giants. He was a unanimous first-team All-American in 1980. As a senior, he recorded sixteen sacks and was named the ACC Player of the Year.

Charlie Justice
Charlie "Choo-Choo" Justice earned his nickname because he looked like a runaway train as he plowed through defenders. He served in the Navy during World War II before entering North Carolina. A single-wing tailback, Justice was the runner-up in the Heisman Trophy voting in both 1948 and 1949. He won the Maxwell Trophy as the nation's best player in 1948.

Michael Jordan
Considered by many as the best player in basketball history, Jordan started his legend as a freshman when he hit the game-winning shot in the 1982 NCAA title game to lift UNC past Georgetown. In his next two years, he was named the National Player of the Year. He went on to a stellar NBA career, which included six NBA championships and six MVP awards with the Chicago Bulls.

James Worthy
Worthy led North Carolina to the 1982 national championship. He was named the National Player of the Year that season. He won three NBA titles with the Los Angeles Lakers and was named the MVP of the 1988 Finals. He is one of four UNC players inducted in the Naismith Memorial Hall of Fame.

Dean Smith

Dean Smith coached North Carolina to 879 wins, retiring in 1997 after 36 years at the helm as the NCAA's all-time wins leader. He guided the Tar Heels to NCAA championships in 1982 and 1993 and led UNC to eleven Final Fours. He was inducted into the Naismith Hall of Fame in 1983.

STADIUM

Kenan Stadium: Since its opening in 1927, North Carolina's Kenan Stadium has offered one of the most beautiful settings for college football in the country. It was named after Frank H. Kenan, a 1935 graduate and the great-great-grandson of General James Kenan, who was a member of UNC's founding board of trustees. The stadium sits in a natural hollow surrounded by Carolina pine trees. There have been several expansions and renovations to Kenan over the years, including the Loudermilk Center for Excellence and a section of premium seating known as the Blue Zone.

NOTABLE ALUMS

Thomas Wolfe
author *Look Homeward, Angel*

Alexander Julian
fashion designer

Andy Griffith
TV star

Jeff MacNelly
creator of the comic strip "Shoe"

ARENA

Dean E. Smith Center: The Dean E. Smith Center opened midway through the 1985-86 season and is named in honor of the legendary coach. The first game at the Smith Center featured No. 1 North Carolina against No. 3 Duke. Both teams were undefeated at the time. North Carolina won 95-92. The Carolina Basketball Museum, which opened its doors in 2008, is housed in the Smith Center complex.

CUSE CONNECTION

ALL-TIME FOOTBALL RECORD VS. SYRACUSE: 2-2

1995: Syracuse 20, North Carolina 9

1996: North Carolina 27, Syracuse 10

2002: North Carolina 30, Syracuse 22

2003: Syracuse 49, North Carolina 47 (3 OTs)

ALL-TIME BASKETBALL RECORD VS. SYRACUSE: 4-3

1957: North Carolina 67, Syracuse 58

1975: Syracuse 78, North Carolina 76

1983: North Carolina 87, Syracuse 64

1983: North Carolina 87, Syracuse 64

1987: Syracuse 79, North Carolina 75

1987: North Carolina 96, Syracuse 93 (OT)

2009: Syracuse 87, North Carolina 71

Donovan's debut: On September 2, 1995, Donovan McNabb started at quarterback for Syracuse. The opponent was the University of North Carolina. The game was in Chapel Hill. It was the first game of McNabb's college career. He would go on to start every game in his four-year Syracuse career. On that September evening, McNabb led Syracuse to a 20-9 victory over the Tar Heels.

Jim Lee's shot: In the 1975 NCAA Tournament, Syracuse upset sixth-ranked North Carolina 78-76 in the East Region semifinals in Providence. The Tar Heels boasted Phil Ford, Mitch Kupchak, and Walter Davis. North Carolina led 76-75 when Syracuse got the ball with twenty-seven seconds remaining. Rudy Hackett found Jim Lee open for an eighteen-foot jumper with five seconds left. Lee buried the shot. Syracuse would go on to its first Final Four appearance in school history.

Boeheim's big win: Jim Boeheim won a lot of games in his first ten seasons as Syracuse's head coach, but critics, including some Syracuse fans, thought that his teams couldn't win the big game. On March 21, 1987, Syracuse faced No. 2 North Carolina in the NCAA's East Region finals at the Meadowlands. Syracuse, led by junior center Rony Seikaly's twenty-six points and eleven rebounds, knocked off the Tar Heels to advance to the Final Four. The Syracuse players carried Boeheim off the court on their shoulders.

MASCOT

While the University of North Carolina's athletic teams go by the Tar Heels nickname, the school's mascot is a ram. The idea came in 1924 when the head cheerleader, Vic Huggins, decided the school needed a mascot, and he seized on the nickname given to Jack Merritt. The star fullback on the 1922 football team had been known as "the Battering Ram."

Rameses the First made his debut on November 8, 1924, as North Carolina took on a heavily favored team from Virginia Military Institute. North Carolina kicker Bunn Hackney was called upon to kick a field goal late in the fourth quarter with the score tied at 0-0. Before he ran onto the field, Hackney stopped to pet Rameses for good luck. He booted the game-winning field goal for a 3-0 victory.

FIGHT SONG

"I'm a Tar Heel Born"

I'm a Tar Heel born

I'm a Tar Heel bred

And when I die, I'm a Tar Heel dead

So it's—Rah, Rah, Carolina-lina

Rah, Rah, Carolina-lina

Rah, Rah, Carolina!

Go to hell, Duke!

OTHER SPORTS

Basketball may be the best-known athletic program at the University of North Carolina, but the most successful is unquestionably women's soccer. Under longtime coach Anson Dorrance, the women's soccer team has won twenty-one NCAA championships, and its long list of standout players includes the legendary Mia Hamm. The women's field hockey team has won six NCAA titles, with the most recent coming in 2009. North Carolina's men's lacrosse team has won four national titles, and the soccer team has two NCAA titles, including the 2011 crown. North Carolina's women's basketball team captured the 1994 NCAA title.

GAME DAY

MEDIA

Broadcasting the Game: WCHL-AM 1360 in Chapel Hill, WRDU-FM 106.1 in Raleigh/Durham.

Covering the Tar Heels: www.newsobserver.com (*Raleigh News & Observer*), www.dailytarheel.com (UNC student newspaper), www.espn.go.com/blog/north-carolina-basketball (ESPN basketball blog)

TAILGATING

Tailgating is allowed, but open flames and alcohol are prohibited. The best options are the PD-Cardinal Deck and the Manning Lot. These have the most available spaces—1,200 and 500, respectively. Cost is eight dollars per car. Go to www.dps.unc.edu for maps and directions to the lots.

There is no public RV parking on campus, but there is free parking for RVs at the Friday Center Park and Ride Lot off of NC Highway 54. Parking in those areas is available beginning at 5 p.m. on the Friday evening preceding football Saturdays. Fans parking at the Friday Center Park and Ride Lot can get to the game by riding the Chapel Hill Transit buses beginning three hours prior to game time. The cost is five dollars per person roundtrip.

SHUTTLE

An alternative to the traditional tailgate is Tar Heel Town, which starts about two and half hours before kickoff with the Old Well Walk, the Kick-off Show, and lots of fan-friendly activities. There are shuttles from Tar Heel Town to Kenan Stadium. Additionally, Chapel Hill Transit provides shuttles from park-and-ride lots throughout Chapel Hill and Carrboro. For more shuttle information, go to www.townofchapelhill.org.

TRADITIONS

Old Well Walk: On football game days, the Tar Heels football team partakes in the Old Well Walk. The Walk starts at the Old Well, one of the most famous campus landmarks. The team walks through the heart of the campus to the Kenan Football Center. The Walk begins approximately two hours and thirty minutes prior to kickoff.

Late Night with Roy: The unofficial start to the basketball season begins with Late Night with Roy. It's a fun-filled version of Midnight Madness with skits that involve the Tar Heel players. The event always plays to a full Smith Center.

ABOUT TOWN

Chapel Hill is located in Orange County. The town does actually sit atop the hill, which was the site of an Anglican chapel built in 1752. The site of the chapel, known as New Hope Chapel, is the current site of the Carolina Inn. Chapel Hill was founded in 1816, mainly to serve the growing University of North Carolina. The town received its chartered in 1851. Chapel Hill has a population of 57,233 (according to the 2010 Census).

RAH, RAH, CAROLINA!

LODGING

The Carolina Inn: Built in 1924 and incorporating eighteenth-century elements of George Washington's Mount Vernon, the Carolina Inn is nestled on the UNC campus. In 1935, the Inn's founder, John Sprunt Hill, donated the hotel to the university with the stipulation that the Inn's profits were to be used to support the university library. The Carolina Inn is listed on the National Register of Historic Places. *211 Pittsboro St., Chapel Hill, NC 27516, 800-962-8519 or 919-933-2001, www.carolinainn.com*

Chapel Hill University Inn: The sports fan's dream hotel. The University Inn, located about three miles from the UNC campus, bills itself as the Home of the Sports Experience. The lobby is adorned with sports paraphernalia, including banners for all the ACC schools. The hotel also offers the Time Out Sports Bar. *1301 North Fordham Blvd. (U.S. Highway 15-501), Chapel Hill, NC 27514, 888-452-5765 or 919-929-2171, www.chapelhilluniversity.com*

EATING

Crook's Corner: Opened in 1978, Crook's Corner traces its roots back to the 1940s when Rachel Crook ran a fish market and café at the exact location. Today, Crook's Corner is known as the birthplace of shrimp and grits, but you'll also want to try the Mount Airy chocolate soufflé cake, Princess Pamela's buttermilk pie, Hoppin' John, and jalapeno hushpuppies. *610 West Franklin St., Chapel Hill, NC 27516, 919-929-7643, www.crookscorner.com*

Mama Dip's: In 1957, Mildred Edna Cotton Council (a.k.a. Mama Dip) opened a tiny takeout restaurant along with her mother-in-law. In 1976, Mama Dip opened her own restaurant. The youngest of seven children, she had learned to cook by watching her older brothers and sisters. The result is real downhome country cooking from the breakfast menu featuring omelets, pancakes, and biscuits to the lunch and dinner fare highlighted by fried chicken, barbeque pork ribs, and catfish. *408 West Rosemary St., Chapel Hill, NC 27516, 919-942-5837, www.mamadips.com*

Top of the Hill Restaurant: Years ago, Top of the Hill was a corner store, a place for UNC students to buy beer and snacks. The restaurant was started to prevent a large chain restaurant from invading the quaint college town. Patrons can start with Franklin Street nachos and then move on to buttermilk fried chicken or French Quarter jambalaya. The restaurant is also well-known for its microbrew pub. *100 East Franklin St., Chapel Hill, NC 27514, 919-929-8676, www.topofthehillrestaurant.com*

SIGHTSEEING

The Carolina Basketball Museum: The state-of-the-art museum is located off the first floor of the Williamson Athletics Center. The museum uses a "Game Day" theme, taking visitors into a theater for the pre-game build-up and then into the main part of the museum with its interactive displays. *450 Skipper Bowles Dr., Chapel Hill, NC 27599, 919-962-6000, www.goheels.com/fls/3350/museum*

Morehead Planetarium & Science Center: The Morehead Planetarium was the first planetarium on a college campus. NASA trained many of its astronauts here. The science center offers activities and programs suitable for all ages. The GlaxoSmithKline Fulldome Theater is the largest fulldome digital video planetarium on a college campus in the world. *250 East Franklin St., Chapel Hill, NC 27599-3480, 919-962-1236, www.moreheadplanetarium.org*

SHOPPING

Johnny T-Shirt: Located in the middle of Chapel Hill's Franklin Street, Johnny T-Shirt offers every piece of Carolina blue memorabilia imaginable. If the Carolina fan can't find what he or she wants here, it doesn't exist. *128 E. Franklin St., Chapel Hill, NC 27514, 919-967-5646, www.johnnytshirt.com*

Julian's: Founded in 1942 by Maurice Julian, the father of famed designer Alexander Julian, the business remains in the family. Find the latest in men's and women's clothing plus accessories. Expect personal service and custom tailoring. *135 East Franklin St., Chapel Hill, NC 27514, 919-942-4563, www.julianstyle.com*

NIGHTLIFE

Cat's Cradle: Since its opening in 1969, Cat's Cradle has become a famous venue for live music. The stage has seen acts from Joan Baez to Nirvana to Iggy Pop to Public Enemy. If you're into music, you have to spend an evening at Cat's Cradle. *300 East Main St., Carrboro, NC 27510, 919-967-9053, www. catscradle.com*

He's Not Here: One of the best-named bars anywhere, He's Not Here is an iconic Chapel Hill drinking establishment. The bar opened in 1973. It includes an open courtyard for warmer evenings. Patrons can purchase a beer in a 33-ounce Carolina blue cup, which they keep as a souvenir. There is live entertainment. *112-½ West Franklin St., Chapel Hill, NC 27516, 919-942-7939*

Four Corners: A Chapel Hill institution located right across Franklin Street from the UNC campus. Named after UNC coach Dean Smith's Four Corners offense, the restaurant boasts sixteen high-definition televisions. It's perfect for dinner or a brew and a game. *175 East Franklin St., Chapel Hill, NC 27514, 919-537-8230, www.fourcornersgrille.com*

LAST-MINUTE TIPS

Where to Shop: University Mall (*201 South Estes Drive at Willow Drive, Chapel Hill*) is Chapel Hill's largest shopping center with sixty stores, including local businesses and national retailers.

Where to Buy Tickets: It's always possible to stroll through the campus in search of tickets. Football games preceded by tailgating offer the perfect opportunity to buy someone else's extra tickets. To ensure your seat, the best way is through websites such as stubhub.com or nctarheelstickets.vividseats.com.

TRAVELING TO CHAPEL HILL?

Chapel Hill is about a thirty-minute drive from Raleigh-Durham International Airport, which services the Research Triangle area. It's about eleven hours from Syracuse to Chapel Hill, nine and a half hours from New York City, and five hours from Washington, D.C.

N.C. State

The North Carolina General Assembly founded a land-grant college in 1887, to be called the North Carolina College of Agriculture and Mechanical Arts.

In 1962, the name was changed to North Carolina State. Now, the Raleigh-based university is the largest school of the state's college system. It still focuses on the liberal and practical educational offerings along with its foundation disciplines of agriculture, life sciences, engineering, design, and textiles.

North Carolina State is part of the famous research triangle of colleges, along with Duke, in Durham, and the University of North Carolina, in Chapel Hill.

The proximity of those three colleges fuels the rabid sports following and rich history of the Wolfpack athletics programs. The first game for the college, though, was on the gridiron against a different local school. The men from A&M, as the college was called, wore pink and blue as they defeated the football squad from the Raleigh Male Academy in 1892 by the score of 12-6. It's said that the players were just getting to know the rules of the game. Indeed, the football team won the school's first conference title, in 1927.

Two years later, the basketball team captured the Southern Conference crown, and the tradition of hoop madness had taken root. Basketball is said to be king on what is called Tobacco Road, and N.C. State has played its important role on the court. The Wolfpack men's basketball history can be neatly broken down into the reigns of its three most successful coaches: Everett Case from 1946 to 1965; Norm Sloan from 1967 to 1980; and Jim Valvano from 1980 to 1990.

Case coached the Wolfpack to six Southern Conference championships in a row and was at the helm for the beginning of the ACC in 1953. The Southern Conference had too many members, and the bigger schools decided to break off and form their own league. So, it was Case's Wolfpack squad that topped Wake Forest in the initial ACC Tournament championship game, earning the sole NCAA Tournament bid that went with it.

Sloan led N.C. State to its first national title. Forward David Thompson, who led that 1974 Wolfpack squad, was argued as the best player in ACC history for more than a decade afterward.

The energetic Valvano coached N.C. State to the 1983 national title. The video clip of Valvano dancing around the court looking for someone to hug after Lorenzo Charles's last-second dunk beat heavily favored Houston is a classic. Valvano has become a folk hero for the courageous and outspoken battle he waged before finally falling to cancer. ESPN still plays that clip of the just-victorious coach, as well as the audio of his speech about not ever giving up in the fight against the disease during the yearly fund-raising period the sports cable giant calls "Jimmy V. week."

The current Wolfpack coach is Mark Gottfried. After N.C. State beat rival Duke when the Blue Devils were ranked No. 1 in the 2012-13 season, joyous Wolfpack fans stormed the court.

In football, the Wolfpack has won the ACC title seven times, including a crown in 1973 under Head Coach Lou Holtz. N.C. State's last ACC title came in 1977, under the direction of Bo Rein.

Running back Ted Brown, quarterback Philip Rivers, defensive lineman Mario Williams, and quarterback Russell Wilson are notable N.C. State players

PROGRAM HIGHLIGHTS

Football

NATIONAL CHAMPIONSHIPS (0): The highest final ranking for the Wolfpack was No. 11 in 1974, when North Carolina State went 9-1-1. The tie came in a 31-31 stalemate vs. Houston in the Astro-Bluebonnet Bowl.

ACC CHAMPIONSHIPS (7): 1957, 1953, 1964, 1965, 1968, 1973, 1979

BOWL RECORD: 14-11-1 (.538). Last bowl—38-24 loss to Vanderbilt in the 2012 Music City Bowl

LONGEST WINNING STREAK: 9 games (three times): 1966-67, 1972-73, 2002

WINNINGEST COACH: Earle Edwards (1954-1970), 77-88-8 (.468)

HEISMAN TROPHY WINNERS OR HIGHEST HEISMAN FINISH: Running back Ted Brown 1978, sixth

Basketball

NATIONAL CHAMPIONSHIPS (2): 1974, 1983

ACC CHAMPIONSHIPS: Regular season (7): 1955, 1956, 1973, 1974, 1985, 1989; Conference tournament (10): 1954, 1955, 1956, 1959, 1965, 1970, 1973, 1974, 1983, 1987

NCAA TOURNAMENT RECORD: 35-23 (.614) Last appearance—Lost 76-72 to Temple in second round of 2013 tournament.

WINNINGEST COACH: Everett Case (1946 to 1964), 377-134 (.738)

NATIONAL PLAYERS OF THE YEAR: David Thompson (1975)

who went to on impressive NFL careers. The Wolfpack earned a bowl bid following the 2010, 2011, and 2012 regular seasons under the direction of Tom O'Brien. But O'Brien was fired before the Music City Bowl. Dave Doeren was hired from Northern Illinois to take over the Wolfpack football program.

LEGENDS

David Thompson

The high-jumping Thompson was one of the first players that truly seemed to defy gravity. His reported forty-eight-inch vertical leap and alley-oop dunks from passes by teammate Monte Towe earned Thompson the nickname of "Skywalker." Thompson led N.C. State to an undefeated regular-season mark of 27-0 in 1973; the following year he led the Wolfpack to its first national championship, defeating UCLA in the title game. That year, he teamed with center Tommy Burleson to beat Maryland 103-100 in an overtime ACC Tournament final some still consider the best ACC Tourney game ever, in part because it came when only the ACC Tourney champ received an NCAA bid. His No. 44 jersey is the only number retired at N.C. State. Thompson went on to become a four-time NBA All-Star with the Denver Nuggets and Seattle SuperSonics.

Dereck Whittenburg/Sidney Lowe/Thurl Bailey

This trio gets listed as one entry because it was the teamwork of these three seniors that brought the Wolfpack to its second national title in 1983. Guards Whittenburg and Lowe were high school teammates under legendary DeMatha coach Morgan Wootten. Forward/center Bailey came from the Washington, D.C., area, too, from Bladensburg High. In the 54-52 victory over Houston in the NCAA title game, it was Whittenburg's too-short jumper gathered in and dunked by Lorenzo Charles as the game-winner. Lowe also went on to coach at N.C. State, compiling a record of 86-78 from 2006 to 2011.

Ted Brown

Brown thrilled Raleigh with a four-year Wolfpack career that saw the running back become the all-time ACC rushing leader, with 4,602 yards. Brown also set the ACC single-game mark, picking up 251 yards on the ground in 1977. The North Carolina native was a consensus All-ACC pick all four of his seasons with the Wolfpack and was a consensus All-American in 1978, too. He was drafted in the first round by the Minnesota Vikings and played eight seasons in the NFL.

Philip Rivers

Quarterback Rivers was a record-breaker at N.C. State, starting fifty-one straight games in his four-year career. He passed for 13,484 yards and 95 touchdowns. Rivers led the Wolfpack to four straight bowl games, winning three of them, including a victory over Notre Dame in the 2003 Gator Bowl. After his senior season, he was named ACC Football Player of the Year and then ACC Athlete of the Year. Rivers was MVP of the 2004 Senior Bowl before going on to a successful career with the San Diego Chargers that has included four Pro Bowl appearances.

NOTABLE ALUMS

General William C. Lee
"Father of the U.S. Airborne"

John Edwards
U.S. senator and two-time presidential candidate

Abdurrahim El-Keib
Interim prime minister of Libya

Rajendra Kumar Pachauri
Chief of Intergovernmental Panel on Climate Change

Zach Galifianakis
Actor

Scotty McCreery
American Idol winner and country singer

ARENA

PNC Arena: On December 2, 1949, the Wolfpack men's basketball team beat Washington & Lee 67-47. Thus began a fifty-year run in the on-campus Reynolds Coliseum as one of the toughest road stops in the nation. In fact, ESPN commentators Jay Bilas (from Duke) and Hubert Davis (from North Carolina) both called the long and narrow Reynolds, with sidecourt seats pressed close to the court, the toughest away arena in the ACC. Alas, the Wolfpack men moved to the brand new PNC Arena, with 10,000 more seats and the amenities of a pro venue, in 1999. (The Wolfpack's successful women's basketball team still plays in Reynolds.) PNC, which calls Carter-Finley and the North Carolina state fairgrounds neighbors, was the second-largest arena in the ACC behind North Carolina's Smith Center. In the upcoming season, though, it will also trail the Carrier Dome and then Louisville's KFC Yum! Center, too.

STADIUM

Carter-Finley Stadium: Carter-Finley Stadium can be considered an almost-campus facility. It's on N.C. State land, but its Trinity Street location is actually a couple miles west of the campus. It opened in 1966 as Carter Stadium, named after two brothers who contributed greatly to its construction, Harry and Nick Carter. The hyphen and Finley were added in 1978 to honor another big donor, Albert Finley. Carter-Finley Stadium has gone through several upgrades. The Vaughn Towers, with club seats and media boxes, opened in 2005.

CUSE CONNECTION

ALL-TIME FOOTBALL RECORD VS. SYRACUSE: 6-0

1972: North Carolina State 43, Syracuse 20

1974: North Carolina State 28, Syracuse 22

1977: North Carolina State 38, Syracuse 0

1978: North Carolina State 27, Syracuse 19

1997: North Carolina State 32, Syracuse 31 (OT)

1998: North Carolina State 38, Syracuse 17

ALL-TIME BASKETBALL RECORD VS. SYRACUSE: 1-4

1990: Syracuse 86, North Carolina State 79 (Big East-ACC Challenge)

2001: Syracuse 54, North Carolina State 53

2001-02: North Carolina State 82, Syracuse 68

2010: Syracuse 65, North Carolina State 59

2011: Syracuse 88, North Carolina State 72

Still an oh-fer: Syracuse carried an all-time mark of 0-5 as the Orange traveled to Raleigh on October 1, 1998, but there were reasons for optimism. Syracuse had lost by a whisper to the Wolfpack in an overtime Carrier Dome game the year prior. Donovan McNabb had quarterbacked the Cuse to a No. 11 AP ranking. Indeed, McNabb's two-yard TD run put Syracuse up 7-0. Alas, it was all N.C. State thereafter, and the fans rushed the field as the Wolfpack made it 6-0 all-time over Syracuse.

Frantic finish: For almost thirty-five minutes, it looked as if the No. 12 Orange was going to fall on February 2, 2001, in Raleigh. They were shooting horribly from the field—just 29 percent in the first half—and trailed the Wolfpack by eleven points with 5:26 left in the game. But Syracuse hit six of eight shots down the end, capped by a layup by Damone Brown with 17.6 seconds left, to beat N.C. State 54-53. Preston Shumpert led the way with twenty-five points, and Syracuse raised its record to 18-3.

Remain undefeated: Syracuse was undefeated and No. 1 in the country for this trip down Tobacco Road on December 17, 2011. The Wolfpack's C.J. Williams led all scorers with twenty-five points, but it wasn't enough to overcome the Orange's veteran leadership. Sixth man Dion Waiters led the Orange with twenty-two points, while Kris Joseph notched twenty-one and Scoop Jardine sixteen as Syracuse prevailed 88-72 and raised its record to 11-0.

MASCOT

The N.C. State teams were known as the Red Terrors until 1921, when an anonymous letter to the student newspaper declared that some football players were as unruly as a pack of wolves. The football squad took the Wolfpack name thereafter; the rest of the school teams were renamed in 1947. The live wolves at games were first known as Lobo. The costumed sideline mascots are Mr. Wuf and Ms. Wuf. In 1981 they were married at a basketball halftime ceremony officiated by Wake Forest mascot the Demon Deacon. Now N.C. State puts a Tamaskan dog on the sidelines, and calls it Tuffy.

FIGHT SONG

"NCSU Fight Song"

Shout aloud to the men

Who will play the game to win

We're behind you

Keep fighting for State

Hold that line

Hold them fast

We will reach victory at last

We're behind you

Keep fighting for State

Rise up to the fray

And let your colors wave

Shout out for dear old State

Go State

For where ever we go

We will let the whole world know

We're behind you

Keep fighting for State

OTHER SPORTS

The Wolfpack baseball team is often ranked nationally. Coached by Eliott Avent since 1997, the Wolfpack plays at Doak Field. The baseball team has made the NCAA Tournament twenty-five times and made the College World Series once, 1968. The Wolfpack has captured the diamond ACC titles four times in the regular season and four times in the ACC Tournament. Also popular are the squads that still call Reynolds Coliseum home, including the women's basketball team and gymnastics squad.

GAME DAY

MEDIA

Broadcasting the Game: WRAL-FM 101.5 in Raleigh

Covering the Wolfpack: www.newsobserver.com (*Raleigh News & Observer*), www.technicianonline.com (N.C. State student newspaper), espn.go.com/blog/ACC (ESPN ACC blog)

TAILGATING

Tailgating is allowed. Good golly, at Carter-Finley Stadium, tailgating is encouraged. Yep. This past season, the Wolfpack held a season-long tailgating competition, selecting the best parties at each home game and bestowing prizes. Beer is allowed, but not in kegs. Everybody is told to carry a picture ID because police and staff check for IDs. Tailgaters are also expected to place their bottles and cans in the designated recycling bins, too. The Carter-Finley lots, with parking for 12,000, open a whopping five hours before game time. Believe it or not, all of these usually go to Wolfpack Club members. The general public is directed to the Vet School lots, which also open five hours prior to game time. Parking fees vary at assorted public and private lots. For information, go to www.gopack.com/travel/parking-maps. Basketball parking is beside PNC Arena, with a cost of $10 per car. Go to thepncarena.com/plan-a-visit/parking-guide.

SHUTTLE

There are several shuttle services that run through the campus and to and from general parking lots, including the Wolfline. For information, go to www2.acs.ncsu.general.edu/trans.

TRADITIONS

Walk of Champions: Wolfpack fans are invited to join the marching band and cheerleaders to wish the football team well as it leaves the football center on Trinity Road to begin its trek to the stadium. The Walk of Champions takes place approximately two hours and thirty minutes prior to kickoff.

See the Memorial Bell Tower: Everybody on the N.C. State campus likes to look up at the Memorial Bell Tower. It was built in 1936 to honor students who gave their lives in service to the country. Most of the time, the tower is lighted in white. But on special campus occasions, the community gathers to watch the light switched to red. And football and basketball Wolfpack victories are counted among those special events.

Krispy Kreme Challenge: Although there may be some sprinting involved, this tradition doesn't really have anything to do with football or basketball game days. It's just, well, pretty different. The KKC began in 2004, as a dozen friends ran from the campus Bell Tower to the the Krispy Kreme Doughnut Shop, wolf(packed) down a dozen donuts and ran back. The distance covered: about five miles. The calories consumed: much more than that. The goal: complete the circuit in less than an hour. The event that started as a dare was turned into a benefit event, and by 2011, 7,500 participated. Think you can break the sixty-minute mark?

ABOUT TOWN

Raleigh is the second largest city in North Carolina, trailing only Charlotte. Its population of nearly 420,000 makes it the forty-second largest city in the United States. But it's so close to Durham and Chapel Hill that the Research

Triangle includes N.C. State, Duke, and the University of North Carolina and is often considered one area, with a population of more than 1.7 million. Raleigh is a tree-filled city, with the nickname "City of Oaks." It takes its name from Sir Walter Raleigh, the English aristocrat and explorer who lived from 1554 to 1618. He popularized tobacco in England, and the sandy soil in North Carolina turned out to be perfect for the crop. Hence the nickname Tobacco Road.

LODGING

DoubleTree by Hilton Hotel Raleigh Brownstone: That's a big name, but this hotel promises to live up to it. It's just three blocks from the N.C. State campus, and close enough to walk to Cameron Village, Pullen Park, and the Glenwood South restaurant and nightlife district. *1707 Hillsborough Rd., Raleigh, NC 27605, 919-828-0811, www.brownstonehotel.com*

Holiday Inn Raleigh: This edition of the popular chain has recently refurbished rooms. It sits close to major shopping at the Crabtree Valley Mall. It's seven miles from the airport and five miles to the campus. There's also Carolina Jack's Steakhouse on the premises. *4100 Glenwood Ave., Raleigh, NC 27612, 919-782-8600, www.hihotelraleigh.com*

EATING

Poole's Diner: John Poole opened his restaurant in 1945 because he loved dessert. The most popular offering was his pies. Soon patrons wanted more, and the "chicken slick" sandwich was born. Nowadays, owner and chef Ashley Christensen runs a joint that's retro chic. Poole's has restored the best of the old style, including the double horseshoe bar and red leather banquettes. Specials are listed on oversized chalkboards. *426 S. McDowell St., Raleigh, NC 27601, 919-832-4477, www.poolesdowntowndiner.com*

18 Seaboard: Chef Jason Smith presides over the restaurant located in the former Seaboard Train Station. He puts out fare considered contemporary Southern. How's a fried green tomato BLT or cornbread-crusted Carolina classics farm catfish sound to you? 18 Seaboard prides itself on local offerings. Its site declares that in January 2013, it purchased $6,426.11 worth of "local products from local purveyors." *18 Seaboard Ave., Raleigh, NC 27604, 919-861-4318, www.18seaboard.com*

Vivace: Fine Italian dining is the fare from the kitchen of executive chef Ian Sullivan. Ever hear of a short rib pizza? It's on the menu, along with lobster risotto, crab-stuffed trout, and porcini dusted beef tenderloin. *4209 Lassiter Mill Rd., Raleigh, NC 27609, 919-787-7747, www.vivaceraleigh.com*

SIGHTSEEING

Duke and UNC: If you're down to see a game at N.C. State, doesn't that make you the kind of sports fan that wants to check off other college sports meccas in addition to Carter-Finley, PNC Arena, and Reynolds Coliseum? A half-hour drive to the southwest will get you to Durham, home to Duke University's Cameron Indoor Stadium basketball gym. Go another ten minutes south from there to the University of North Carolina with the new (Smith Center), old (Carmichael Auditorium, now named Carmichael Arena and home to the Tar Heels women's basketball team), and stadium-in-the-pines (Kenan).

North Carolina Museum of History: In the early 1880s, *Raleigh News and Observer* publisher Samuel A'Court proclaimed that there seemed to be a story worth preserving everywhere he looked around Raleigh. City editor Frederick Augustus Olds agreed. The North Carolina Museum of History was born not only of their ideas, but their efforts, too. Today it's proudly proclaimed as "The People's Museum," with exhibits tied to the history of those tied to the state. *5 E. Edenton St., Raleigh, NC 27601, 919-807-7850, ncmuseumofhistory.org*

SHOPPING

Raleigh State Farmers' Market: The place to buy fresh is open seven days a week. Visitors can delight in locally grown produce of all types. But there's more, including restaurants and shops that also cater to the local—wine, candles, picture frames, soaps, lotions, and more. *1201 Agriculture St., Raleigh, NC 27603, 919-733-7417, www.ncagr.gov/markets/facilities/markets/raleigh*

The Tarlton: Raleigh's shop local, buy local includes this building that's home to a pair of unique shops. Cat Banjo features jewelry and items that promote rescue dogs. Its neighbor is the Revolver Consignment, with its ever-revolving collection of vintage and cool clothing and more. If it's the right day, American Meltdown: Gourmet Melts will be there. That's the name of one of Raleigh's most popular food trucks, owned by friends of the aforementioned. *122-126 Glenwood Ave., Raleigh, NC 27603, shoplocalraleigh.org*

NIGHTLIFE

Tir Na Nog Irish Pub: This joint bills itself as Raleigh's first true Irish pub. Its site proudly declares that it's been "pulling pints" since 1997. Like Syracuse's Kitty Hoynes, Tir Na Nog features Irish food and music, too. By the way, the name means "land of eternal youth." *218 S. Blount St., Raleigh, NC 27601, 919-833-7795, www.tirnanogirishpub.com*

Zydeco Downtown: The Big Easy meets downtown Raleigh. You can eat gumbo for lunch and dinner, listen to live music from Wednesday to Saturday nights, and soak up the hip atmosphere. Not exactly Bourbon Street, but with a Hurricane in your hand . . . *208 Wolfe St., Raleigh, NC 27601, 919-834-7987, www.zydecodowntown.com*

Irregardless Cafe: It's a restaurant, music joint, and bar all in one. The food is green . . . yeah, salads, but more, in tune with what's healthy and sustainable. The music is jazzy. The bar . . . well, the place boasts the Raleigh "server of the year." *901 W. Morgan St., Raleigh, NC 27603, 919-833-8898, www.irregardless.com*

LAST-MINUTE TIPS

Where to Shop: Hillsborough Street borders the campus to the north. It's full of eateries, T-shirt shops, and, yes, bars. The N.C. State campus is dry, so fans are likely to hang out on Hillsborough Street.

Where to Buy Tickets: A walk on the wild side of Hillsborough might be the answer to ticket needs, too. The Wolfpack has its own page on stubhub.com.

TRAVELING TO RALEIGH?

Raleigh is about a fifteen-minute drive from Raleigh-Durham International Airport, which services the Research Triangle area. It's about ten hours from Syracuse to Raleigh, nine hours from New York City, and five hours from Washington, D.C.

Notre Dame

On November 26, 1842, the University of Notre Dame sprang from the mind of French priest Reverend Edward Sorin. Sorin and seven companions stood on 523 acres in the Indiana mission fields and decided to construct a university. Sorin named it, in his native tongue, *L'Universite de Notre Dame du Lac*, a tribute to Our Lady of the Lake. In 1844, the university received its charter from the state of Indiana.

In 1879, fire ruined the main building, which, indeed, was the home to most of the campus activity. Sorin took that as a sign. He had built his vision too small. "We will rebuild it bigger and better than ever," Sorin declared. And now Notre Dame is arguably the most well-known university in the world.

A lot of the credit goes to its historic sports programs, particularly the Fighting Irish football.

Notre Dame lost its first-ever football game, 8-0, to Michigan in 1887. The Fighting Irish went on from there to win eleven national titles.

The tradition lays claim to Knute Rockne, the coach who led Notre Dame

UNIVERSITY OF NOTRE DAME

STUDENTS
11,731

SOUTH BEND
pop. 101,168

NOTRE DAME STADIUM
80,795

EDMUND P. JOYCE CENTER
9,149

COLORS
Gold & Blue

NICKNAME
Fighting Irish

MASCOT
Leprechaun

CAMPUS ATTRACTIONS
Sacred Heart Basilica,
Our Lady of Lourdes Grotto,
Touchdown Jesus

PHONE
574-631-5000
(general information)

574-631-5555
(campus police)

574-631-6107
(athletic department)

TICKETS
574-631-7356 or
www.und.com

to a winning percentage of .881 from 1918 to 1930. The Rockne era birthed the legend of the Four Horsemen, the rock-solid nickname bestowed upon the 1924 backfield of quarterback Harry Stuhldreher and backs Jim Crowley, Elmer Layden, and Don Miller by noted sportswriter Grantland Rice. Then came the "win one for the Gipper" speech, in which Rockne recalled the final words of George Gipp, who died in 1920 of strep throat. After Rockne delivered the halftime inspiration in 1928, Notre Dame rallied to beat Army 12-6.

The Fighting Irish success continued through eras ushered by Frank Leahy, Ara Parseghian, Dan Devine, and Lou Holtz. Current coach Brian Kelly is working hard to reclaim that kind of glory. Last season, the Irish was undefeated until it lost the National Championship Game to Alabama.

Through it all Notre Dame has enjoyed the rooting of what is called the Subway Alumni, a term for Catholics from around the country that started pulling for the Fighting Irish when Notre Dame football was broadcast nationally every Saturday on the radio. Speaking of exclusivity, as Notre Dame and the ACC prepare to enter into their partial-member football partnership, the Fighting Irish is still the only college to have its own over-the-air network contract, with NBC.

Notre Dame has achieved a share of success on the basketball court, too.

The Fighting Irish won two Helms Foundation National Championships before the start of the NCAA Tournament, in 1927 and 1938.

In the modern era, Notre Dame's most recognizable two achievements came under Coach Digger Phelps. In 1974, the Fighting Irish ended UCLA's record winning streak at eighty-eight games. In 1978, Notre Dame made the Final Four.

During the twenty-season Phelps era, from 1971 to 1991, his squads beat the No. 1 team in the nation eight times on the way to a record of 393-197, a winning percentage of .666.

Syracuse fans know current coach Mike Brey well, as his teams have battled Jim Boeheim's squads feverishly as members of the Big East. Since 2000, Brey's winning percentage is better than .660.

Football

NATIONAL CHAMPIONSHIPS (11): 1924, 1929, 1930, 1943, 1946, 1947, 1949, 1966, 1973, 1977, 1988

ACC CHAMPIONSHIPS (0):

BOWL RECORD: 15-17 (.468). Last bowl—Lost 42-14 to Alabama in 2013 National Championship Game

LONGEST WINNING STREAK: 23 games (1988-89)

WINNINGEST COACH: Knute Rockne (1918-1930), 105-12 (.880)

HEISMAN TROPHY WINNERS (7): Angelo Bertelli (1943), Johnny Lujack (1947), Leon Hart (1949), Johnny Lattner (1953), Paul Hornung (1956), John Huarte (1964), Tim Brown (1987)

Basketball

NATIONAL CHAMPIONSHIPS (2): 1927, 1938

ACC CHAMPIONSHIPS (0):

BIG EAST CHAMPIONSHIPS (1): Regular-season title, 2001

NCAA TOURNAMENT RECORD: 31-37 (.456) Last appearance—Lost 76-58 to Iowa State in the first round of the 2013 tournament.

WINNINGEST COACH: Digger Phelps (1971-1991), 393-197 (.666)

NATIONAL PLAYERS OF THE YEAR (3): John Moir (1936), Austin Carr (1971), Adrian Dantley (1976)

LEGENDS

Paul Hornung

The sandy-haired Hornung picked up the nickname "The Golden Boy" on the way to winning the Heisman Trophy in 1956. Hornung was a true two-way player, leading the Fighting Irish offense as a quarterback who could run, pass and kick. Playing safety on defense, Hornung was adept at breaking up passes and was second on the squad in interceptions. He is the only player ever to win the Heisman after playing for a losing team, as Notre Dame was 2-8 that season. The outspoken Hornung went to a Hall-of-Fame career with the Green Bay Packers and was NFL MVP in 1961. He was suspended for a whole season along with fellow star Alex Karras for betting on NFL games.

Tim Brown

Brown earned the nickname "Touchdown Timmy" on the way to becoming the first wide receiver ever to win the Heisman Trophy, in 1987. Indeed, he scored twenty-two TDs in his four years at Notre Dame, and was even more prolific in the NFL. Brown was drafted in the first round, No. 6 overall, by the Oakland Raiders. He scored 105 NFL TDs during a career that saw him make the Pro Bowl nine times.

Austin Carr

They could have named the shooting guard position after Austin Carr. Man, could the 6-foot-4 guard from Washington, D.C., shoot. In his three years for the Fighting Irish, Carr averaged 34.5 points per game. He scored an NCAA Tournament–record sixty-one points in a game vs. Ohio University and averaged fifty points in seven NCAA Tournament games. In 1971, Carr won the National Player of the Year Awards given out by the Helms Foundation, the Naismith Trophy organization, AP, and UPI. Carr went on to play for the Cleveland Cavaliers. He was an NBA All-Star in 1974 and won the J. Walter Kennedy Award for Citizenship in 1980. A decade in Cleveland earned Carr the nickname "Mr. Cavalier."

Adrian Dantley

Rugged forward Dantley came out of the DeMatha High School program coached by legend Morgan Wootten ready for big things at Notre Dame. As a freshman he was an important part of the Fighting Irish team that snapped UCLA's record eighty-eight-game winning streak. Dantley was a consensus All-American two times. He averaged 30.4 points per game in 1974-75 and 28.6 points per game in 1975-76 while also leading Notre Dame in rebounding both seasons. Dantley was named the U.S. Basketball Writers Association's Player of the Year in 1976, a year that also included his role as leading scorer for the U.S. Olympic Team that took the gold medal in Montreal. Dantley was NBA Rookie of the Year for the Buffalo Braves and became a six-time All-Star during a much-traveled career, with the longest stay with the Utah Jazz.

ARENA

Edmund P. Joyce Center: The Notre Dame basketball arena began its life in 1968 with the name Athletic and Convocation Center. The Fighting Irish beat No. 1 UCLA in the building in 1971 as Austin Carr and mates handed the Bruins their only loss of the season. The arena was the site of the Bruins' next loss, in 1974, when Dwight Clay hit the buzzer beater that snapped UCLA's eighty-eight-game win streak. Notre Dame has won 77 percent of its games in the arena. In 1977, NBC named the Notre Dame student body as most valuable player after the Fighting Irish beat No. 1 San Francisco.

In 1987, the arena was named the Edmund P. Joyce Center after the retiring reverend.

STADIUM

Notre Dame Stadium: Notre Dame Stadium opened in 1930, and architects patterned it after Michigan Stadium, but on a smaller scale. It held 54,000 fans. Capacity was increased to around 59,000 by making the seats narrower. Then in 1997, 21,000 seats were added, making Notre Dame Stadium one of college football's big boys, with room for more than 80,000. The stadium is well known for the mural called "Touchdown Jesus." The official name of the painting by Millard Sheets is "The Word of Life." It was installed in 1964 on the wall of Hesburgh Library overlooking the stadium.

CUSE CONNECTION

A big gift from Syracuse: One of Notre Dame's award-winning All-Americans went to South Bend from his hometown of Syracuse. Walt Patulski was a three-sport star in football, basketball, and track and field at Syracuse's Christian Brothers Academy. As a 6-foot-5 fullback, Patulski scored 140 points while leading the Brothers to a 7-1 record in his senior season, 1967. Notre Dame made Patulski a linebacker. And, oh, what a defensive force he was. Patulski started every game of his Notre Dame career, and he won the Lombardi Trophy in 1971, and finished ninth in the Heisman Trophy voting. He returned to upstate New York after being the first-round draft pick of the Buffalo Bills in 1972 and played in the NFL until 1977. Patulski was inducted into the Greater Syracuse Sports Hall of Fame in 1991.

Challenging a loss: Notre Dame came out ahead 17-15 on the scoreboard on November 18, 1961, in Notre Dame Stadium. But the last two plays of the game left a bitter taste for Syracuse players and fans. As time expired, Notre Dame kicker Joe Perkowski missed a fifty-six-yard attempt. But the Orange's Walt Sweeney was flagged for roughing Perkowski. Officials marched off fifteen yards, and, with the clock showing 0:00, Perkowski kicked a forty-one-yarder to put Notre Dame up 17-15. League officials from the Big Ten and ECAC consulted with NCAA officials for days afterward as some newspaper articles claimed Syracuse was wronged and others supported the Fighting Irish's victory. In the end, nobody would overturn the referee's decision on the field that led to Notre Dame's victory.

A victory taken for Granted: In this corner, Syracuse had freshman Jerami Grant. In that corner, Notre Dame had sophomore Jerian Grant. The younger son of former NBA forward Harvey Grant won the battle. Jerami, moved into a starting role with the suspension of teammate James Southerland, played all forty minutes on February 4, 2013, in the Carrier Dome. He scored fourteen points, his best yet for the Orange. Yeah, Jerian led Notre Dame with fifteen, but Syracuse won 63-47.

MASCOT

The Leprechaun stalks the sidelines, shaking his shillelagh and leading the cheers. That's the tradition of the Fighting Irish since 1965. The Notre Dame logo even features the Leprechaun in profile, fists up and ready to take on all comers. But in the wayback machine, Notre Dame's game-day mascot was an Irish terrier dog. The first one was named Brick Top Shaun-Ri. Then the pooch became known as Clashmore Mike. The Leprechaun has proved to be more fitting to dancing an Irish jig and coaxing cheers out of a student section that's become known as the Leprechaun Legion.

OTHER SPORTS

The Subway Alumni make sure that Notre Dame has a big following no matter the sport. Syracuse fans, though, will take particular note of the men's lacrosse team. The Fighting Irish, under Coach Kevin Corrigan, will bring a history of twenty-first-century success with them when they join the Orange in the ACC. Notre Dame was national runner-up, falling to Duke in the NCAA Tournament title game in 2010 and also won its way to the Final Four in 2001 and 2012. And the two schools have been rivals in the Big East Conference's official lacrosse conference since it started in 2010.

FIGHT SONG

"Victory March"

Rally sons of Notre Dame

Sing her glory and sound her fame

Raise her Gold and Blue

And cheer with voices true

Rah Rah for Notre Dame

We will fight in every game

Strong of heart and true to her name

We will ne'er forget her

And we will cheer her ever

Loyal to Notre Dame

Cheer cheer for old Notre Dame

Wake up the echoes cheering her name

Send a volley cheer on high

Shake down the thunder from the sky!

What though the odds be great or small

Old Notre Dame will win over all

While her loyal sons are marching

Onward to victory

GAME DAY

MEDIA

Broadcasting the Game: WSBT-AM 960 and FM 96.1 in South Bend

Covering the Fighting Irish: www.southbendtribune.com (*South Bend Tribune*), www.chicagotribune.com (*Chicago Tribune*), www.ndsmbobserver.com (Notre Dame student newspaper), espn.go.com/blog/notre-dame-football (ESPN football blog)

TAILGATING

Tailgating is encouraged. Grills are allowed, but gas only, with propane tanks limited to twenty pounds. Beer is allowed, but no kegs. Portable sound systems are allowed. Throwing a football is allowed. Public parking will be directed to the Notre Dame Golf Course, with a charge of $40 per car, or the White Field lot, with a charge of $25 per car. The golf course will not be open for parking if it's raining or snowing. The lots open at 8 a.m. Attendants will help multiple-car caravans park together as long as they arrive at the same time. For information, go to gameday.nd.edu/campus/tailgating and gameday.nd.edu/campus/parking.

SHUTTLE

Around campus, pedal cab service and courtesy car service are available. There is no shuttle service from the golf course. There is shuttle service from the White Field lot, and it starts when the lot opens and runs until an hour after the game. For information, go to gameday.nd.edu/campus/campus-transportation-program.

TRADITIONS

Spirit of the Band: The Band of the Fighting Irish does not wait until game day to start spreading music and cheer. The tradition begins at 4 p.m. Friday with Trumpets Under the Dome. The band then plays at 6 p.m. to kick off the pep rally outside the Main Building. The Drummers Circle ends it all at midnight, again under the Golden Dome. On game day, the band, cheerleaders, and the Leprechaun entertain ninety minutes before game time outside Bond Hall. Inside Notre Dame Stadium, you will hear the band play the famous "Notre Dame Victory March" when it takes the field.

Feel Like the Players: On every home game Football Friday, Notre Dame officials open up the stadium from 10 a.m. to 5 p.m. for a Tunnel Tour. Yes, they escort fans through the very entrance the Fighting Irish players have taken to the field for eighty years. From 10 a.m. to 2 p.m. on Football Saturday, they open up the LaBar Practice Field, which is actually three fields, two FieldTurf, and one natural grass.

ABOUT TOWN

South Bend is the fourth largest city in Indiana, with a population of 101,168. It was settled by fur traders in the nineteenth century, and the St. Joseph River was an attraction then and still is. The city sits on the river's southernmost

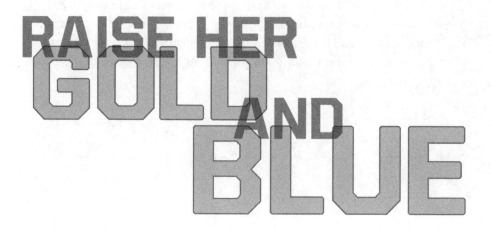

bend; hence the name South Bend. South Bend is the closest city to the Michigan state line on Indiana State Route 31. The general area is sometimes called the Michiana region.

LODGING

Fairfield Inn & Suites at Notre Dame: The hotel is across the street from campus, within walking distance of Notre Dame Stadium. Guests park for free in the hotel lot, and officials know what Saturdays are for during football season. They've set up a barbecue and tailgating area in the hotel lot. *1220 East Angela Blvd., South Bend, IN 46617, 574-234-5510, www.marriott.com/hotels/ travel/sbnd-fairfield-inn-and-suites-south-bend*

Varsity Clubs of America: This hotel features all suites. Although it sits in neighboring Mishawaka, it advertises itself as being "in the heart of a college town." Lots are set up with barbecues for game day, and the hotel also features the Stadium Sports Bar. *3800 N. Main St., Mishawaka, IN 46545, 574-277-0500, www.diamondresorts.com/varsity-clubs-of-america-south-bend*

Rent a house or stay at a bed and breakfast: Some visitors prefer to rent a whole house or stay in somebody else's house in and around South Bend. There's a site set up to help those folks, and it's owned and operated by Notre Dame alumni. rentlikeachampion.com

EATING

Maury's Pat's Pub: Why two first names? In 1969, Pat Perri and his wife opened Pat's Colonial Pub. When they decided it was time to retire in 1990, they decided to sell it to a loyal and regular customer who promised to keep the tradition. That would be Maurice T. Cocquyt. It's fine dining with a Notre Dame theme. The site declares, "Thank you! And Go Irish!" *901 W. 4th St., Mishawaka, IN 46544, 574-259-8282, mauryspatspub.com*

Bruno's Pizza: Bruno's has been serving the Notre Dame area pizza since 1975. Locals love it so much that now there are three South Bend locations, a dozen in northern Indiana, and one southern Michigan franchise. The newest is at *4503 Ameritech Rd., South Bend, IN 46628, 574-247-9999, brunospizza. com*

Rocco's Restaurant: When a restaurant has lasted since 1951, that says something. At Rocco's of South Bend, the message is love—of family, of friends, and of great Italian food. The Verteramo family calls it Italian comfort food. *537 N. Saint Louis Blvd., South Bend, IN 46617, 574-233-2464*

SIGHTSEEING

Spiritual landmarks: You don't have to be Catholic to appreciate the beauty of the religious landmarks throughout the Notre Dame campus. The Sacred Heart Basilica is open for masses on Fridays and Saturdays. The Grotto of Our Lourdes is open at all times, with everybody invited to light a candle. And the mural known as "Touchdown Jesus" was designed to honor "Christ the Teacher." In addition, there are pieces of art placed all around campus that invite people to sit and pray, or perhaps just stand and reflect about life. gameday.nd.edu/experience/spiritual

Walk the trails: The Notre Dame campus contains trails that include two rivers: the St. Joseph's and the St. Mary's. Bring a camera. They are beautiful. Maps are available at the Eck Visitors Center. *112 N. Notre Dame Ave., South Bend, IN 46637, 544-631-5000, www.nd.edu/visitors*

SHOPPING

Downtown South Bend: The downtown area has everything a strolling visitor might seek. Boutiques. Antiques. Eateries. Newsstands. Clothing stores. Highlights include the CircaArts Gallery and the Center for History. Go to www.downtownsouthbend.com.

University Park Mall: They call this a super-regional mall because it serves northern Indiana and southern Michigan. It's part indoor, part outdoor, and includes 124 stores and restaurants. *6501 Grape Rd., Mishawaka, IN 46545, 574-271-5531, www.simon.com*

NIGHTLIFE

Linebacker Lounge: The Linebacker Lounge was founded in 1962 by former Notre Dame football player Myron Pontios and local businessman Stan Pisek. Today it's owned by Elwanda "Al" Delinski, and it's still considered one of *the* Fighting Irish hangouts. There are fifteen flat-screen TVs to go along with a bar-staple menu and drink specials. *1631 South Bend Ave., South Bend, IN 46617, 574-289-0186, www.backer-nd.com*

Corby's Irish Pub: Folks rave about this Irish Pub's pizza, especially the Italian sausage pizza. Corby's features a big bar room that was used in the filming of *Rudy*, and an outdoor beer garden, too. *441 E. Lasalle Ave., South Bend, IN 46617, 574-233-5326, www.facebook.com/corbysirishpub*

Fiddler's Hearth: A true Celtic pub in the heart of Fighting Irish country. The owners, Carol, Patrick, and Sean Meehan, invite the world in "for a pint, a dram, a plate, and a song." That means you can drink, eat, and listen to Irish music, not necessarily in that order. *127 N. Main St., South Bend, IN 46601, 574-232-2853, www.fiddlershearth.com*

LAST-MINUTE TIPS

Where to Shop: The Notre Dame campus is well prepared to sell you just what you wanted to take home as a souvenir. There are six official locations on game day: the Hammes Notre Dame Bookstore, Varsity Shop I on the second-floor shop at Joyce Center, the Leep Varsity Shop 2, the Adidas Tent on the Irish Green, the Irish Express at LaFortune Student Center, and the Golf Shop on Warren Golf Course.

Where to Buy Tickets: Notre Dame Stadium is a tough ticket. The school makes visitors show tickets before they're allowed into lots on game day. You can stroll around campus looking for sellers, or get cracking way ahead of time on the secondary sale sites like stubhub.com and vividseats.com, both of which have Notre Dame pages.

TRAVELING TO SOUTH BEND?

The Notre Dame campus is about a fifteen-minute drive from South Bend Regional Airport. It's about two hours from Chicago's O'Hare and ninety minutes from Chicago's Midway. A drive from Syracuse to South Bend would take about nine hours, fifteen minutes.

Pitt

The University of Pittsburgh traces its origins to 1787 when the Pittsburgh Academy opened in a log cabin near Pittsburgh's three rivers. In 1819, the school's name changed to Western University of Pittsburgh, and in 1908, the school officially became known as the University of Pittsburgh.

In 1926, Pittsburgh chancellor John Bowman commissioned work on the Cathedral of Learning. The project was finished in 1937. The Gothic-style tower is the second-tallest education building in the world, standing forty-two stories and just over five hundred feet tall. The cathedral was partially funded by 97,000 area school children, each of whom contributed a dime to buy a brick for the building. It remains the geographic and traditional heart of the Pitt campus.

The university sits on 132 acres in the Oakland section of Pittsburgh, adjacent to the 456-acre Schenley Park. Originally, a private school, Pittsburgh became state-related in 1966.

Pittsburgh fielded its first intercollegiate football team in 1890, when the university

UNIVERSITY OF PITTSBURGH

STUDENTS
28,823

PITTSBURGH
pop. 334,563

HEINZ FIELD
65,050

PETERSEN EVENTS CENTER
12,508

COLORS
Blue & Gold

NICKNAME
Panthers

MASCOT
Roc the Panther

CAMPUS ATTRACTIONS
The Cathedral of Learning, Heinz Chapel, Allegheny Observatory

PHONE
412-624-4141
(general information)

412-624-2121
(campus police)

412-648-8230
(athletic department)

TICKETS
800-643-PITT or
www.pittsburghpanthers.com/tickets/pitt-tickets.html

was still known at Western University of Pittsburgh. The program can boast a rich and successful history that includes names such as Pop Warner, Mike Ditka, and Tony Dorsett.

Glenn "Pop" Warner, whose name is now synonymous with youth football, became Pitt's head coach in 1915. He won his first thirty games at Pitt, going undefeated in 1915, 1916, and 1917. He remained at Pitt for nine years, winning 81.6 percent of his games.

In 1924, Dr. John B. "Jock" Sutherland took over as the Panthers' head coach. He would become Pitt's all-time winningest coach with a career record of 111-20-12. Sutherland guided Pitt to the Rose Bowl in 1927, 1929, and 1932. Pitt lost each time. But in 1936, Pitt capped an 8-1-1 season with a 21-0 Rose Bowl win over Washington. The 1937 team repeated as national champion with a 9-0-1 record, with the tie coming in a 0-0 deadlock with Fordham's famous Seven Blocks of Granite team.

In 1976, Johnny Majors coached the Panthers, featuring the Heisman Trophy-winning Tony Dorsett, to a 12-0 record and the national championship. Pitt defeated Georgia, 27-3, in the Sugar Bowl to cap the perfect season. Perhaps the best team in Pitt history, the 1980 squad finished 11-1 with only a road loss to Florida State.

Over the years a host of legendary players have donned the blue and gold uniform. Joe Schmidt, Hugh Green, Mark May, and Dan Marino are among the many who have had their numbers retired.

Pittsburgh's basketball program dates back to 1905. The school, however, discontinued basketball after the 1907-08 season. After two years with no team, the school brought back the sport in 1910. One year later, Dr. George M. Flint took over as head coach and remained at the helm for the next ten years, leading the Panthers to eight winning seasons. One of Flint's players was H.C. "Doc" Carlson.

Andrew Kerr succeeded Flint as Pitt's head coach, but after just one season, the job went to Carlson. He would go on to become Pitt's all-time winningest coach. He served as head coach from 1922 to 1953, and he guided the Panthers to two Helms Foundation national titles—in 1927-28 and 1929-30. The 1927-28 squad went 23-0 and remains the only team in Pitt history to go undefeated. In 1941, Pitt beat North Carolina to advance to the Final Four where the Panthers lost to eventual national champion Wisconsin. Carlson is a member of the Naismith and Helms Foundation Halls of Fame.

In 1955, Julius Pegues became the first African-American to play

Football

NATIONAL CHAMPIONSHIPS (9): 1915, 1916, 1918, 1929, 1931, 1934, 1936, 1937, 1976

BIG EAST CHAMPIONSHIPS (2): 2004, 2010

BOWL RECORD: 12-17 (.413). Last bowl—28-6 loss to SMU in 2012 BBVA Compass Bowl

LONGEST WINNING STREAK: 30 games, 1916 to 1918

WINNINGEST COACH: John "Jock" Sutherland (1924-38), 111-20-12 (.818)

HEISMAN TROPHY WINNERS OR HIGHEST HEISMAN FINISH: Running back Tony Dorsett, 1976 winner

Basketball

NATIONAL CHAMPIONSHIPS (0): The Panthers lost to Wisconsin in the 1941 championship game. Prior to the NCAA Tournament, Pitt was named national champion by the Helms Foundation in 1929 and 1930.

BIG EAST CHAMPIONSHIPS (6): 1987, 1988, 2002, 2003, 2004, 2011

BIG EAST TOURNAMENT CHAMPIONSHIPS (2): 2003, 2008

NCAA TOURNAMENT RECORD: 23-25 (.479). Last appearance—73-55 loss to Wichita State in the first round of the 2013 tournament

WINNINGEST COACH: H.C. "Doc" Carlson (1922-53), 367-248 (.596)

NATIONAL PLAYERS OF THE YEAR: Charley Hyatt, 1930

basketball at Pitt. He led the 1957 team to the school's second NCAA Tournament appearance. As a senior in 1958, he helped the Panthers return to the tournament.

Like Pitt football, the basketball program has produced a slew of great players, including Billy Knight, Charles Smith, Clyde Vaughn, and Brandin Knight. Perhaps the greatest player in Pitt history is Charley Hyatt, a member of the undefeated 1928 team and an inductee in both the Naismith and Helms

Foundation Halls of Fame. Hyatt was the National Player of the Year in 1930.

After five years as a member of the Eastern 8, Pittsburgh joined the Big East Conference in 1982. The move lifted Pitt basketball to another level. Since 1985, Pitt has had ten players nominated a total of thirteen times for the Wooden Award. Recent coaches Ben Howland and Jamie Dixon have both been honored as the National Coach of the Year. The Panthers went to the NCAA Tournament ten straight times between 2002 and 2011.

LEGENDS

Tony Dorsett
One of the best running backs in college football history, Tony Dorsett was a three-time All-American at Pitt. He finished fourth in the Heisman Trophy balloting in 1975 before winning the award in 1976. He led the Panthers to the 1976 national championship. He's one of just two players to win the Heisman Trophy, a collegiate national championship, a Super Bowl championship, and be elected into both the college and pro football halls of fame.

Dan Marino
In his college career, Dan Marino led Pitt to four consecutive top ten finishes. In his sophomore year, Marino guided the 1980 Panthers to a No. 2 final ranking. He finished his career as Pitt's all-time leader in passing yards and completions, and he still holds the school's records for touchdown passes in a career and a season. He has been inducted into the college and pro halls of fame.

Mike Ditka
Before he became a Super Bowl-winning coach with the Chicago Bears and a noted ESPN analyst, Mike Ditka starred as a pass-catching tight end for the Pittsburgh Panthers. Ditka played at Pitt from 1958 to 1960. He led Pitt in receiving all three years and was a unanimous All-American in 1960. He played baseball and basketball at Pitt and was also the school's intramural wrestling champion. He went on to a stellar career with the Chicago Bears and Dallas Cowboys. He's enshrined in the college and pro halls of fame.

Charles Smith

A quarter century after finishing his career at Pittsburgh, Charles Smith remains the Panthers' all-time scoring leader. He scored 2,045 points in his career, which spanned from 1984 to 1988. He still ranks second in career rebounds. In his last two years, Smith helped Pitt to a combined record of 49-16 and a pair of Big East championships. He was the third overall pick in the 1988 NBA Draft.

STADIUM

Heinz Field: The University of Pittsburgh plays its home football games at Heinz Field, which is also the home of the NFL's Pittsburgh Steelers. The Panthers began playing at Heinz Field in 2001. The stadium is situated at the tip of the city at the convergence of the famous three rivers. The pro facility provides the Panthers with tremendous amenities, including a 28 × 96-foot video board, three club lounges, 129 suites, and over 7,000 club seats. In addition, the stadium has 500 televisions linked to the main video board.

NOTABLE ALUMS

Gene Kelly
Academy Award-winning dancer, actor, and singer

Mark Cuban
owner of the NBA's Dallas Mavericks

Fred Rogers
host of *Mister Rogers' Neighborhood* television show

Jonas Salk
developer of the polio vaccine

Benjamin Spock
author of several child development books

ARENA

Petersen Events Center: The Panthers unveiled their basketball palace in 2002. The Petersen Events Center boasts one of the best basketball environments in the country. The arena's amenities include courtside suites, a restaurant row, and a four-sided video board. In addition to the basketball arena, the facility also features the Panthers Hall of Champions, an auxiliary basketball practice court, a student recreation center, and athletic training areas. The Panthers won 132 of their first 143 games at the arena.

OTHER SPORTS

Pittsburgh's first football game was played in 1889, but the first intercollegiate sport played at Pittsburgh was baseball. The team, called the University Nine, debuted in 1869. Pittsburgh's track and field program has produced several All-Americans, including Olympic gold medalist John Woodruff and Roger Kingdom, a two-time gold medal winner in the 110-meter hurdles. The wrestling program boasts sixteen individual NCAA champions. Pitt's men's swimming team has won nineteen Big East titles, while the women's program has nine conference championships. The women's volleyball team has won eleven Big East titles since joining the conference in 1983.

CUSE CONNECTION

Pitt snaps SU's streak: Pittsburgh ended the longest winning streak in Syracuse history on October 29, 1960. The Orangemen were national champions in 1959 with an 11-0 record and were off to a 5-0 start to the 1960 season when Pittsburgh staged a 10-0 upset at Syracuse's Archbold Stadium. The sixteen straight wins remains the longest winning streak in Syracuse history.

The Patterson brothers: Perry Patterson played football at Syracuse from 2003 to 2006. He was a three-year starter at quarterback. Patterson ranks fourth in school history in career pass attempts (862) and career completions (456) and fifth in passing yards (5,220). His brother, Lamar, plays basketball at Pittsburgh. Lamar Patterson, a 6-foot-5 wing, will be a senior at Pitt during the 2013-14 season.

Bob and Bobby Lazor: Bob Lazor played basketball at Pittsburgh from 1954 to 1957. As a senior, Lazor helped the Panthers to the second NCAA Tournament appearance in school history. Pitt went 16-11 that season. The Panthers defeated Morehead State in the first round of the NCAA tourney before losing to Kentucky, 98-92, in the Mideast Regional semifinals. He still ranks seventh on Pitt's career rebound list despite having just three varsity seasons and is twenty-fourth in career scoring with 1,175 points. Lazor's son, Bobby, played at Syracuse for two years in the mid-1990s before transferring to Arizona State.

MASCOT

The University of Pittsburgh chose the Panthers as its mascot back in 1909, but the mascot's origins are unclear. The school's website lists five different reasons for the choice:

1. The formidable creature was once indigenous to the Western Pennyslvania region;
2. The panther has a noble standing;
3. The happy accident of alliteration;
4. The panther's golden hue is a close approximation to Pitt's color of old gold;
5. At the time, no other college or university used the Panther nickname.

The mascot's name is Roc in honor of a former Pitt football player and coach named Steve Petro. Petro played on Pitt's national championship team in 1937. He played pro football, served in the army, and then returned to Pitt, where he coached or worked in the athletic department from 1950 to 1984. He was known as "the Rock upon which Pitt football grew," hence, the mascot's nickname—Roc.

FIGHT SONG

"Victory Song"

Let's go Pitt, we're set for victory

So lend a hand, strike up the band!

Let's go Pitt, we're making history

We'll never yield out on the field.

The whistle blows, we're on our toes

The ball is IN the air.

It may be rough the going tough

But always fighting fair so . . .

(Chorus) Fight on for dear old Pittsburgh

And for the glory of the game

Show our worthy foe that the Panther's on the go

Pitt must win today! Rah! Rah! Rah!

Cheer loyal sons of Pittsburgh

Cheer on to victory and fame

For the Blue and Gold shall conquer as of old

So fight, Pitt, fight!

Da da da da da-da Fight, Pitt, fight!

Da da da da da-da Fight, Pitt, fight!

V-I-C-T-O-R-Y!

GAME DAY

MEDIA

Broadcasting the Game: WDKA-FM 93.7 in Pittsburgh, WRIE-AM 1260 in Erie, and WTKT-AM 1460 in Harrisburg

Covering the Panthers: www.post-gazette.com (*Pittsburgh Post-Gazette*), www.pittsburghlive.com (*Pittsburgh Tribune-Review*)

TAILGATING

Tailgating is permitted in the parking lots surrounding Heinz Field. The University of Pittsburgh sanctions several pre-game activities, including the Great Lawn Tailgate and the World's Largest Family Tailgate. The Panther Prowl begins approximately three hours before kickoff. The Pitt Band puts on a pre-game concert. Parking lots around the stadium open five hours before game time. Information on specific game-day activities can be found at Pitt's Game Day Central at www.pittsburghpanthers.com.

SHUTTLE

One of the best ways to arrive at Heinz Field is via the Gateway Clipper. Fans can board the riverboats at Station Square as early as two hours before kickoff. The shuttles return to Station Square up to thirty minutes after the game ends. The cost is just ten dollars roundtrip and kids six and under ride free.

If you prefer to go by land rather than sea, fans can park downtown and ride the Port Authority's "T" for free. The cost of parking downtown, at the First Avenue Garage or the Mellon Garage, is just five dollars. Both are close to "T" Stations.

TRADITIONS

Sweet Caroline: Traditions don't have to be old to be worthwhile. One of Pitt's best traditions started in 2008. At football games, the Pitt students sing the Neil Diamond classic "Sweet Caroline" at the end of the third quarter. The tradition started at the Pitt-Buffalo game on September 26, 2008. Later that season, the Pitt band played it on the road at Notre Dame Stadium. The Panthers were behind after three quarters but came back to tie the game and sent it into overtime, where they beat the Fighting Irish. A tradition was born.

The Cathedral Victory Lights: Whenever Pittsburgh wins a football game, the lights at the top of the Cathedral of Learning are lit. The glow can be seen from all across the Pitt campus. The tradition started with football, but it has since spread to other sports and includes accomplishments such as winning conference and national championships.

ABOUT TOWN

The Allegheny and Monongahela rivers meet to form the Ohio River. Pittsburgh's famous three rivers have played a huge role in the city's history, from its beginnings to the modern age. Early French and British explorers realized the strategic importance of the three rivers. The two countries fought

for control of the region in the 1750s. When the War of 1812 cut off British supplies from the region, Pittsburgh began to grow as a manufacturing city. Pittsburgh first began producing steel in 1875. In the early 1900s, half of America's steel came from Pittsburgh's mills. Pittsburgh's economy sagged as the steel industry dipped. Within the past decade the city has re-made itself into a cultural, technological, and educational hub.

LODGING

Holiday Inn-University Center: There are several hotels near the University of Pittsburgh's campus, including the Holiday Inn-University Center. The hotel is within walking distance of Carnegie Mellon. *100 Lytton Avenue, Pittsburgh, PA 15213, 412-682-6200, www.holidayinn.com/hotels/us/en/ pittsburgh/pitsp/hoteldetail*

Fairmont: The Fairmont soars above the Pittsburgh skyline, offering incredible views of PNC Park and the city's downtown. It is centrally located to restaurants, shopping, and entertainment. *510 Market Street, Pittsburgh, PA 15222, 412-773-8800, www.fairmont.com/pittsburgh/*

Omni William Penn: The William Penn, built in 1916, remains one of Pittsburgh's best-known luxury hotels. The huge lobby is right out of a movie set. It's located in downtown Pittsburgh within an easy walk of the Pittsburgh Cultural District, the Strip District, and more. *530 William Penn Place, Pittsburgh, PA 15219, 412-281-7100, www.omnihotels.com/FindAHotel/ PittsburghWilliamPenn.aspx*

EATING

Primanti Bros.: Ask any Pittsburgher where to get something to eat that you can't get anywhere else and the answer will be Primanti's. At Primanti's, the "Almost Famous" sandwich menu includes the iconic marriage of sandwiches with French fries wedged inside, between the bread and the meat. Today, there are dozens of Primanti's located all over the Pittsburgh area, but the second-oldest shop is in the Oakland section near the university. *3803 Forbes Avenue, Pittsburgh, PA 15213, 412-621-4444, www.primantibros.com*

Pamela's Diner: Pamela's P&G Diner is a Pittsburgh institution. The restaurant regularly wins awards for best breakfast in Pittsburgh. The pancakes are the reason. They're a cross between the traditional flapjack and a crepe. They come in a host of varieties, including banana walnut and banana chocolate chip. There will be a wait, so get there early! *3703 Forbes Avenue, Pittsburgh, PA 15213, 412-683-4066, www.pamelasdiner.com*

Joe Mamas: Joe Mamas Italian Deluxe restaurant is owned and operated by Joseph Michael Mama, who, according to the restaurant's website, was a first-generation member of an Italian-American immigrant family and learned everything he knows about cooking from his mom and his *nonna* (that's Italian for grandma). Joe's has a broad menu and the prices are modest. You can get the four-cheese ravioli for just $9.95, and the highest-priced menu item is the bacon-wrapped center-cut sirloin with sautéed mushrooms and Gorgonzola for just $18.95. *3716 Forbes Avenue, Pittsburgh, PA 15213, 412-621-SAUC, www.joemamas.com*

SIGHTSEEING

Mount Washington and the Duquesne Incline: One of Pittsburgh's most iconic features is the cable-car inclines that take riders from the edge of the Ohio and Monongahela rivers to the top of the bluffs overlooking the city. Catch the Duquesne Incline at Station Square and ride it to Mount Washington. *USA Today* rated the view from the top of Mount Washington as the second-most beautiful in the United States. *Station Square, 125 West Station Square Drive, Pittsburgh, PA 15219, 412-381-1665, www.stationsquare. com/info/inclines*

Carnegie Museums of Art & Natural History: These two distinct museums are in the same location. The Carnegie Museum of Art was founded by industrialist and philanthropist Andrew Carnegie in 1895. It is nationally and internationally recognized for its distinguished collection of American and European works from the sixteenth century to the present. The Museum of Natural History is ranked among the top five natural history museums in the country. It features twenty exhibition halls. *4400 Forbes Avenue, Pittsburgh, PA 15213, 412-622-3131, web.cmoa.org and www.carnegiemnh.org*

SHOPPING

Carson Street Shopping District: A wide variety of stores and shops can be found in this south side neighborhood. From the eco-friendly products at E House Company to everything that is denim at the Pittsburgh Jean Company, unique items make this a fun area to visit.

The Strip District: The Strip is a half-mile square area northeast of downtown Pittsburgh. The area is brimming with ethnic food stores, restaurants, and coffee shops, and there is a wide selection of retail stores and craft boutiques. The Strip even has its own website: www.neighborsinthestrip.com.

NIGHTLIFE

Fat Heads Saloon: The menu at Fat Heads features something called Headwiches, which are huge creations. Imagine the Southside Slopes, which consists of kielbasa topped with fried pierogies, American cheese, grilled onions, and horseradish sauce. In addition, Fat Heads offers burgers, wings, and ribs plus forty-two craft-brewed beers. *1805 East Carson Street, Pittsburgh, PA 15203, 412-431-7433, www.fatheadspittsburgh.com*

LAST-MINUTE TIPS

Where to Shop: The Waterfront is a retail store center that's closest to the Pitt campus. There are clothing stores, department stores, restaurants, and hotels. *149 W. Bridge Street, Homestead, PA 15120, www.waterfrontpgh.com*

Where to Buy Tickets: Local ticket brokers can be hit or miss. It's best to go with a national ticket broker such as stubhub.com or www.vividseats.com.

Peter's Pub: Located near the University of Pittsburgh campus, Peter's Pub is a destination post-game bar. It's a sports bar and more, offering live music, food that's not your average bar food fare, and an impressive selection of imported beers. *116 Oakland Avenue, Pittsburgh, PA 15213, 412-681-7465, www.my-peterspub.com*

Hemingway's Café: Another great hangout near the Pitt campus is Hemingway's. The menu consists of the usual sandwiches, burgers, and pizza to an entrée selection that includes chicken marsala and salmon picatta. There are over twenty beers on tap. *3911 Forbes Avenue, Pittsburgh, PA 15213, 412-621-4100, www.hemingways-cafe.com*

TRAVELING TO PITTSBURGH?

There are no direct flights from Syracuse to Pittsburgh; however, there are several flights from Eastern hubs such as Washington, D.C., Philadelphia, and New York's LaGuardia Airport. It takes approximately six hours to drive from the Salt City to the Steel City.

Syracuse

SYRACUSE UNIVERSITY

STUDENTS
13,987

SYRACUSE
pop. 141,683

CARRIER DOME (FOOTBALL)
49,262

CARRIER DOME (BASKETBALL)
35,012

COLORS
Orange

NICKNAME
Orange

MASCOT
Otto

CAMPUS ATTRACTIONS
Hendricks Chapel
Hall of Languages
Carmelo K. Anthony
Basketball Center

PHONE
315-443-1870
(general information)

315-443-2224
(campus police)

315-443-8705
(athletic department)

TICKETS
888-DOME-TIX or
www.carrierdome.com/tickets

In February of 1870, at the Methodist State Convention in Syracuse, a resolution was passed to found a university. The Reverend Jesse T. Peck, who was elected president of the Syracuse University Board of Trustees, suggested purchasing fifty acres of farmland in southeastern Syracuse. The Board of Trustees drew up a charter on March 24, 1870, and approved it one day later.

The cornerstone for the university's first building, the Hall of Languages, was laid in August of 1871, but rather than wait for construction, the Board of Trustees rented space in a building in downtown Syracuse and opened the College of Liberal Arts in September of that year.

In May of 1873, the Hall of Languages was dedicated. In the next twenty years, the university built and opened the Holden Observatory, a law college, and the college of medicine.

Syracuse University played its first football game on November 23, 1889. Syracuse, wearing pink and blue uniforms, lost to Rochester 36-0 in that season's only game. The following year, Syracuse adopted orange as the school's official color. Syracuse went 8-3 in 1890 as Bobby Winston became the school's first head football coach.

In 1905, John D. Archbold gave the university money to build its first football stadium. Archbold Stadium, a 20,000-seat approximation of the Roman Coliseum, opened on September 25, 1907, as Syracuse defeated Hobart 28-0. In 1915, Syracuse went 9-1-2 and earned an invitation to the Rose Bowl, but the school had to decline the invitation because an earlier trip to the West Coast to play Oregon State had used up the team's travel budget.

In 1938, Wilmeth Sidat-Singh, an African-American whose stepfather was Hindu, played quarterback for Syracuse and led the team to a 5-3 record. After five straight losing seasons, Syracuse hired Ben Schwartzwalder as head coach. He would take the program to unprecedented heights. He coached the likes of Jim Brown, Ernie Davis, Floyd Little, and Larry Csonka. The 1959 team went undefeated, beat Texas in the Cotton Bowl, and was crowned national champion.

In recent years, Syracuse has continued to produce All-Americans, including Art Monk, Tim Green, Don McPherson, Dwight Freeney, and Donovan McNabb.

Syracuse's men's basketball program traces its roots back to 1900-01, one year after the school's first women's team played. Archbold Gym opened in 1909 and remained the home of Syracuse basketball until 1962, although it was almost completely destroyed by a fire in 1947. In the early years, Syracuse's greatest player was Vic Hanson, a three-sport star who led the basketball team to a 19-1 record in 1926. Syracuse's best teams took on the names the Reindeer Five and the S Men. In the 1940s, Billy Gabor became Syracuse's best player, setting a record for scoring that would remain until the legendary Dave Bing arrived in 1962. One of Bing's teammates was a bespectacled kid from Lyons, N.Y., named Jim Boeheim. Boeheim played at SU, returned as an assistant coach, and in 1976 took over as head coach. Boeheim has become the face of Syracuse basketball, recording over 900 career wins in 37-plus years.

In Boeheim's tenure, Syracuse has moved from intimate Manley Field House to the cavernous Carrier Dome. What was once a modestly successful Eastern school is now a national power.

The program boasts star players like Pearl Washington, Derrick Coleman,

PROGRAM HIGHLIGHTS

Football

NATIONAL CHAMPIONSHIPS (1): 1959

BIG EAST CHAMPIONSHIPS (4): 1996, 1997, 1998, 2004

BOWL RECORD: 14-9-1 (.583). Last bowl—A 38-14 win over West Virginia in the 2012 Pinstripe Bowl

LONGEST WINNING STREAK: 16 games (1959-1960). Syracuse went 11-0 in 1959 and then won the first five games of the 1960 season before losing to Pittsburgh.

WINNINGEST COACH: Floyd "Ben" Schwartzwalder (1949-73), 153-91-3 (.626)

HEISMAN TROPHY WINNERS OR HIGHEST HEISMAN FINISH: Running back Ernie Davis in 1961

Basketball

NATIONAL CHAMPIONSHIPS (3): Syracuse won the 2003 NCAA title. Syracuse was also named national champion in 1918 and 1926.

BIG EAST CHAMPIONSHIPS (10): 1980, 1986, 1987, 1990, 1991, 1998, 2000, 2003, 2010, 2012

BIG EAST TOURNAMENT CHAMPIONSHIPS (5): 1981, 1988, 1992, 2005, 2006

NCAA TOURNAMENT RECORD: 60-36 (.625) Last NCAA appearance—A 61-56 loss to Michigan in the Final Four of the 2013 tournament

WINNINGEST COACH: Jim Boeheim (1976-present), 890-304 (.745)

NATIONAL PLAYERS OF THE YEAR: Derrick Coleman in 1990

Lawrence Moten, and Gerry McNamara. Boeheim guided Syracuse to the NCAA championship game in 1987 and 1996, and in 2003 the Orange, led by Carmelo Anthony, finally won its first national title. In 2013, Syracuse returned to the Final Four for the fifth consecutive decade.

LEGENDS

Jim Brown
Brown played at Syracuse from 1954 to 1956. He still holds the school records for most rushing touchdowns in a game (six) and most points scored in a game (forty-three). As a senior, he led Syracuse to the Cotton Bowl. He was one of SU's best athletes ever, as he played basketball and lacrosse as well. He went on to play for the Cleveland Browns and is still considered by many as the NFL's best running back of all-time. He's a member of both the Pro and College halls of fame.

Ernie Davis
Davis followed in Jim Brown's footsteps. In 1959, Davis scored two touchdowns as Syracuse defeated Texas in the Cotton Bowl to cap off its undefeated national championship season. In 1961, Davis became the first African-American to win the coveted Heisman Trophy. He died of a rare form of cancer before ever getting the chance to play in the NFL. The movie *The Express* is based on his life.

Dave Bing
Syracuse had one of the worst basketball programs in the country when Dave Bing arrived in 1962 from Spingarn High School in Washington, D.C. Bing resurrected the Syracuse program. His freshman team beat the school's varsity. In his three varsity seasons, Bing led the Orangemen to three consecutive winning records and a combined record of 52-24. As a senior, Bing helped Syracuse to the NCAA's East Region finals. He finished his career with 1,883 points, which remained the school's record for twenty-three years until Sherman Douglas broke it in 1989. Bing, who spent twelve years in the NBA and is now the mayor of Detroit, is a member of the Naismith Memorial Hall of Fame.

Carmelo Anthony
In 2003, Carmelo Anthony delivered a long-awaited NCAA championship to Syracuse's fans. In his one and only year at Syracuse, Anthony was a consensus All-American and a first-team All-Big East selection. He averaged 22.2 points and 10.0 rebounds per game. Both are school records for a freshman. He was the No. 3 pick in the 2003 NBA draft, and he's been a member of the past three U.S. Olympic teams.

ARENA

From 1962 to 1980, Syracuse played its basketball games in Manley Field House, where the dusty floor and a raucous student section known as the Manley Zoo created a hostile environment for opposing teams. Syracuse won fifty-seven consecutive games at Manley, a streak that was broken in the final game at Manley when Georgetown stunned Syracuse.

In 1980, Syracuse moved into the cavernous Carrier Dome. At first, Syracuse coach Jim Boeheim balked at the idea of losing his home-court advantage at Manley Field House, but eventually the Carrier Dome became one of the most iconic venues in all of college basketball.

Syracuse plays to huge crowds each year. Syracuse has led the nation in attendance twelve times and finished no lower than fourth in its thirty-two years in the Dome. On February 23, 2013, the largest crowd in Dome history—35,012 fans—saw Georgetown beat Syracuse, 57-46, snapping the Orange's thirty-eight-game home winning streak.

NOTABLE ALUMS

Joe Biden
Vice president of the United States

Eileen Collins
First female space shuttle commander

Bob Costas
Sports broadcaster

Vanessa Williams
Recording artist and actress

STADIUM

Carrier Dome: The Carrier Dome was built between 1979 and 1980 to replace Syracuse's archaic Archbold Stadium. Syracuse played all of its home games during the 1979 season in alternative venues, including Cornell University and the Buffalo Bills' stadium.

The Carrier Dome cost $26.85 million, which included a $2.75 million gift from the Carrier Corporation for the stadium's naming rights. Ironically, though named for an air conditioning company, the Carrier Dome is not air-conditioned.

The first football game played in the Carrier Dome was on September 20, 1980. Syracuse defeated visiting Miami (Ohio), 36-24, in front of 50,564 fans.

The Dome's main feature is the Teflon-coated roof, which spans 6.5 acres. The roof consists of sixty-four fiberglass panels and a system of cables. The current roof was installed in 1999 at a cost of $14 million. A total of sixteen electric fans, each measuring five feet in diameter, circulate air into the building and keep the Dome's roof inflated.

TRADITIONS

#44: The number 44 at Syracuse University is one of the most storied numbers ever associated with a college football program. Since 1954, eleven players have worn the number and three earned All-American honors. Those three—Jim Brown, Ernie Davis, and Floyd Little—rank among the finest running backs ever to play the college game.

The university officially retired the No. 44 on November 12, 2005. A jersey bearing the number hangs from the Carrier Dome's rafters, and the 44-yard line is outlined on the Dome's field. The last player to wear No. 44 for the SU football team was Rob Konrad in 1998.

The Varsity: Not only is The Varsity one of the most popular eating establishments on the Syracuse campus, it is also home to one of the oldest traditions at the university. In addition to pizza, sandwiches, and chicken wings, The Varsity features pennants for each of Syracuse's football opponents. When Syracuse wins a game, the pennant of that particular opponent is unceremoniously turned upside down and hung back up on the wall of The Varsity.

FIGHT SONG

"Down the Field"

Down, down the field goes
old Syracuse,
Just see those backs hit the line
and go thro'
Down, down the field they go
marching, Fighting for the Orange
staunch and true.
Rah! Rah! Rah!
Vict'ry's in sight for old Syracuse,
Each loyal son knows she
ne'er more will lose,
For we'll fight, yes. we'll fight,
and with all our might
For the glory of Syracuse.

MASCOT

Otto the Orange, Syracuse's mascot, is one of the most recognizable creatures in college athletics. He is a regular in those ESPN commercials, having been boxed by Charlie Steiner and wired-up to gauge the hit of a bull. But Otto is a relatively recent addition to Syracuse sports.

The first mascot at Syracuse University was the Saltine Warrior, which was spawned by an Indian figure named Big Chief Bill Orange. In a hoax story published in *The Syracuse Orange Peel* in 1931, the remains of a sixteenth-century Onondagan chief were supposedly found in the excavations for the new women's gymnasium. A Saltine Warrior statue still sits near SU's Shaffer Art Building.

The use of an Indian for a mascot met with disapproval from local Native Americans and a Native American student organization. A Roman gladiator was briefly used. In the 1970s and 1980s, mascots ranged from Egnaro the Troll, a man in an orange tuxedo, and a superhero-like figure.

Eventually, the Orange made its appearance. In 1990, the name Otto was given to the fuzzy fruit. In 1995, Otto had to fend off a movement to find a new mascot. Suggestions included a wolf and a lion. The students who served as Otto successfully campaigned to keep Otto.

OTHER SPORTS

Aside from basketball and football, Syracuse University is best known for its lacrosse program. The Syracuse lacrosse team can boast fifteen national championships—four USILA championships in the 1920s and eleven NCAA champions from 1983 to the present. Syracuse lacrosse rose to greatness in the 1980s and 1990s under Coach Roy Simmons Jr., who played at Syracuse for his father, Roy Sr. The younger Simmons played with the likes of Jim Brown and Oren Lyons. Syracuse's five most recent titles came under the guidance of John Desko, a former SU player and assistant to Simmons.

GAME DAY

MEDIA

Broadcasting the Game: WTKW-FM 99.5 and WTLA-FM 97.7 in Syracuse

Covering the Orangemen: www.syracuse.com (*Syracuse Post-Standard*)

TAILGATING

The area around campus is congested, making it difficult to find tailgating spots unless you are a season-ticket holder. Parking lots around the Carrier Dome are used for tailgating. In Armory Square, the Trolley Lot is large enough to accommodate RVs. The Skytop area also offers more space for the out-of-town tailgater.

SHUTTLE

There are shuttles that run from the Skytop area and Manley Field House parking lots. In addition, there are shuttles that run from Armory Square in downtown Syracuse up to the campus.

DOWN, DOWN THE FIELD GOES OLD SYRACUSE

ABOUT TOWN

Named after a city in Italy, the village of Syracuse was officially incorporated in 1825, but the region's history dates back much farther. The Five Nations of the Iroquois Confederacy included the Onondagas, who lived in the area near Onondaga Lake and in the valley south of the lake. In the 1600s, the Onondagas repelled a French invasion led by Samuel de Champlain. In the 1700s, the British cultivated a relationship with the Onondagas through trade.

The region is located in the bed of an ancient sea, and the advent of the Erie Canal grew the salt industry and Syracuse's economic importance. In the 1800s, Syracuse became a key stop in the Underground Railroad. The house of Harriet Tubman is located in nearby Auburn, New York. The salt industry began to wane after the Civil War, and Syracuse, relying on the Erie Canal and the railroad, turned into a center of industry and manufacturing.

In the twentieth century, Syracuse was home to major operations for General Motors, Chrysler, Carrier Corporation, and General Electric. The area is well known for its beauty with the Finger Lakes and the Adirondacks within a few hours drive. The region is also known for its snowy winters, a source of pride for Central New Yorkers, who refuse to let a few feet of snow bother them.

LAST-MINUTE TIPS

Where to Shop: Marshall Street is located right on the edge of the Syracuse campus between University and Irving. The area contains many different shops, bookstores, eateries, and bars.

Where to Buy Tickets: The best place to find tickets is at www.dometix. com, but ticket brokers such as seatgeek and stubhub.com sometimes offer better seats, especially for SU basketball games.

LODGING

The University Sheraton: The Sheraton Syracuse University Hotel & Conference Center is located in the middle of the Syracuse University campus. It's a block from the shops and bars of Marshall Street and just a three-point shot from the Carrier Dome. Book early, though, because the hotel is sold out on most football weekends. *801 University Ave., Syracuse, NY 13210, 315-475-3000, www.sheratonsyracuse.com*

Genesee Grande: Located at the foot of the Syracuse campus, the Genesee Grande puts visitors close to the university's attractions but far enough away to relax amid the koi pond and the welcoming atmosphere of this hotel. In addition to its well-appointed guest rooms, the Genesee Grande also offers luxurious suites. *1060 East Genesee St., Syracuse, NY 13210, 315-476-4212, www.geneseegrande.com*

The Sherwood Inn: Built as a stagecoach stop in 1807, the Sherwood Inn is located in the heart of the historic village of Skaneateles, which is about twenty minutes west of Syracuse. The inn overlooks the northern tip of beautiful Skaneateles Lake. The bed & breakfast–style inn has a main dining room and a lively pub. *26 West Genesee St., Skaneateles, NY 13152, 315-685-3405 or 800-374-3796, www.thesherwoodinn.com*

EATING

Dinosaur Bar-b-Que: The Dinosaur began in 1983 as three partners started a mobile concession unit, serving barbeque out of a fifty-five-gallon drum at motorcycle rallies. In 1988, the Dinosaur opened as a lunch counter operation in downtown Syracuse. Two years later, an expansion brought about a full bar, full-service dining and live music. The rest is finger-licking history. The Dinosaur offers ribs, pulled pork sandwiches and other slow-cooked delicacies as good as anywhere in the country. *246 West Willow St., Syracuse, NY 13202, 315-476-4937, www.dinosaurbarbque.com*

Joey's: If you come to Syracuse, you've got to have a nice Italian dinner. There are many places in the area to choose from, but none better than Joey's Restaurant at Carrier Circle in East Syracuse. Joey's offers fine Italian dining in a warm atmosphere. For a more casual experience, there is Pronto Joey's, which is located upstairs at the same location. *6594 Thompson Rd., East Syracuse, NY 13206, 315-432-0315, www.joeysitalianrestaurant.com*

Scotch 'N Sirloin: The Scotch 'N Sirloin Steakhouse has been an Upstate New York landmark for over forty years. The Scotch 'N Sirloin offers premium steaks and seafood in a welcoming dining room. Before your meal, relax in the hearth-warmed lounge with its peanut shell–covered floor. *3687 Erie Blvd. East, Syracuse, NY 13214, 315-446-1771, www.scotchnsirloin.com*

SIGHTSEEING

Everson Museum of Art: The Everson Museum of Art is located in downtown Syracuse. It was designed by the noted architect I.M. Pei. The museum boasts a significant collection of ceramics plus a pioneering art video collection. *401 Harrison St., Syracuse, NY 13202, 315-474-6064, www.everson.org*

Rosamond Gifford Zoo: The Rosamond Gifford Zoo is a jewel located in Burnet Park, which overlooks the city of Syracuse. The zoo's programs with Asian elephants and Siberian tigers are internationally recognized. The zoo boasts over seven hundred animals on forty-three acres. The outdoor walking trail puts visitors in close proximity to the animals in their natural habitats. *One Conservation Place, Syracuse, NY 13204, 315-435-8511, www. rosamondgiffordzoo.org*

Erie Canal Museum: The Erie Canal Museum is located in the only remaining weighlock building in America. In the 1800s, weigh-houses were part of the canal system and were used to weigh barges to calculate tolls. The canal once ran right through downtown Syracuse. The museum opened in 1962. It details the Erie Canal, which was vital to America's economic growth. *318 Erie Blvd. East, Syracuse, NY 13202, 315-471-0593, www.eriecanalmuseum.org*

SHOPPING

Syracuse Bookstore: The official Syracuse campus bookstore is located in the Schine Student Center. The store has everything from T-shirts to books and assorted other Orange paraphernalia. *900 South Crouse Ave., Syracuse, NY 13244, 315-443-9900, www.bookstore.syr.edu*

Destiny USA: A few minutes from the Syracuse campus, Destiny USA is one of the largest malls in America. Destiny USA consists of more than two hundred retail stores, a movie theater complex, entertainment options including a go-kart track, a comedy club, and WonderWorks. A recent expansion brought in several new restaurants including the Melting Pot, P.F. Chang's, and Texas de Brazil steakhouse. *One Destiny USA Dr., Syracuse, NY 13204, 315-466-6000, www.destinyusa.com*

NIGHTLIFE

Armory Square: The Armory Square district is situated in downtown Syracuse and boasts shops, bars, and restaurants. It's easy to spend an afternoon there in the little boutique shops, then have dinner at Pastabilities or the Empire Brewing Company and move on to the many pubs such as P.J.'s or the Blue Tusk. And before you leave, check out the monument to the 24-second shot clock, which was the brainchild of former Syracuse Nats owner Danny Biasone and got its start in Syracuse. *www.armorysquare.com*

Tipperary Hill: Also known as Tipp Hill, this area of the city was populated back in the day by Irish immigrants, many from the County Tipperary. It's now home to Burnet Park, the Rosamond Gifford Zoo, a thriving neighborhood, and many distinctive pubs. Get a burger at the Blarney Stone. Check out the upside-down traffic light at the corner of Milton Avenue and Tompkins Street. And end the day at Coleman's Authentic Irish Pub, Tipp Hill's most iconic restaurant and bar.

TRAVELING TO SYRACUSE?

Syracuse is served by Hancock International Airport, about eight miles north of the SU campus. Rail and bus lines come into one station at the Regional Market, which is next to the Destiny USA mega-mall and between the campus and the airport. Syracuse is about a four-hour drive northwest from New York City and a six-hour drive north from Washington, D.C.

Virginia

UNIVERSITY OF VIRGINIA

STUDENTS
21,106

CHARLOTTESVILLE
pop. 43,511

SCOTT STADIUM
61,500

JOHN PAUL JONES ARENA
14,593

COLORS
Orange & Navy Blue

NICKNAME
Cavaliers

MASCOT
Cavalier on Horseback

CAMPUS ATTRACTIONS
The Lawn,
the Rotunda

PHONE
434-924-0211
(general information)

434-924-7166
(campus police)

434-982-5000
(athletic department)

TICKETS
800-542-8821 or
www.virginiasports.com

The University of Virginia has presidential roots. The campus in Charlottesville was the brainchild of Thomas Jefferson. It sits on land once owned by James Monroe. Its first Board of Visitors included Jefferson, Monroe, and James Madison.

The Commonwealth of Virginia chartered the University of Virginia on January 25, 1819. In the next century, Franklin D. Roosevelt visited the 1940 commencement to watch son Franklin D. Roosevelt Jr. graduate. FDR delivered the commencement address.

With such a rich history, it's the only U.S. college designated as a World Heritage Site by the United Nations Educational, Scientific and Cultural Organization.

Every student who studies at UVa, as it's usually called, is aware of that Jeffersonian past. The architecture is most impressively represented by the Rotunda, inspired by the inspiration of the Pantheon in Rome, and half its height and width. It sits on one edge of The Lawn, the green space recommended by Jefferson that's surrounded by academic buildings and residence halls.

Jefferson wanted his university to educate future leaders in practical affairs and public service. It was the first university in the country to use the elective system in course studies. Today, UVa carries a top academic reputation, rated the No. 2 public university and No. 24 overall in the *U.S. News and World Report* rankings.

In athletics, the charter member of the ACC interestingly carries more than one nickname. The teams are officially known as the Cavaliers. Students and diehard fans have long also called them the Wahoos, or Hoos for short.

Go ahead, ask. What's a Wahoo? So many people inquire that the UVa includes it on its Frequently Asked Questions page.

The answer: Washington & Lee baseball fans called Virginia players Wahoos during the fierce rivalry of the 1890s. Virginia fans turned the derogatory into a term of endearment. Student newspaper writers shortened it for headline space.

The Cavaliers/Wahoos/Hoos success in sports has come relatively late in school history. Sixteen of UVa's twenty-one national championships came after 1980. Syracuse fans will note that the most successful Cavaliers sport is men's lacrosse, with seven of those national crowns.

The men's basketball team has won five ACC regular-season titles—the first in 1981.

The football team never qualified for a bowl game before 1984. It has played in eighteen since. Befitting that success, UVa has expanded its football venue, Scott Stadium, to fit more than 60,000, and opened John Paul Jones Arena, with a capacity of almost 15,000, to take the place of cozier University Hall, which fit 8,300.

Mike London has coached the football team since 2010, and Tony Bennett took over the basketball program in 2009.

Football

NATIONAL CHAMPIONSHIPS (0): Virginia shared the ACC championship twice, with Duke in 1989 and with Florida State in 1995.

ACC CHAMPIONSHIPS (2): 1989, 1995

BOWL RECORD: 7-11 (.388). Last bowl—43-24 loss to Auburn in the 2011 Chick-fil-A Bowl

LONGEST WINNING STREAK: 10 games (twice), 1914-15 and 1951-52

WINNINGEST COACH: George Welsh (1982-2000), 134-86-3 (.600)

HEISMAN TROPHY WINNERS OR HIGHEST HEISMAN FINISH: Quarterback Shawn Moore, fourth, 1990; Halfback Bill Dudley, fifth, 1941; wide receiver Herman Moore, sixth, 1990

Basketball

NATIONAL CHAMPIONSHIPS (0): Virginia reached the Final Four twice, in 1981 and 1984.

ACC CHAMPIONSHIPS (5): 1981, 1982, 1983, 1985, 2007

ACC TOURNAMENT CHAMPIONSHIPS (1): 1976

NCAA TOURNAMENT RECORD: 22-17 (.564) Last appearance—Lost 71-43 to Florida in the first round of the 2012 tournament.

WINNINGEST COACH: Terry Holland (1974 to 1990), 326-174 (.652)

NATIONAL PLAYERS OF THE YEAR: Ralph Sampson (1981, 1982, and 1983)

LEGENDS

Ralph Sampson

It was a game-changer for the Cavaliers when the 7-foot-4 center out of Harrisonburg, Virginia, ended a fierce recruiting battle by choosing his home state college. Sampson continued to be a publicity magnet, making Virginia one of the most talked-about teams in the ACC from 1979 to 1983. His scoring, rebounding, and shot-blocking helped UVa to the NIT title his freshman year, the NCAA Final Four his sophomore year, and the NCAA Elite 8 his senior year. He won the Naismith Award for player of the year his final three seasons at Virginia. Sampson was a *Sports Illustrated* cover boy five times during his Cavaliers career and again after being drafted No. 1 overall by the Houston Rockets. Sampson won Rookie of the Year and was a four-time All-Star before being slowed by knee surgeries. Funny thing, though. Plenty of people considered Sampson a failure because he did not lead Virginia to the national title.

Bill Dudley

Dudley was just a sixteen-year-old in Bluefield, Virginia, when he was offered a scholarship to attend Virginia to become a placekicker and punter. His sophomore season, he also became a halfback. Big things were to come. Dudley led the Southern Conference in total yards his junior year. After his senior season in 1941, Dudley won the Maxwell Award and was a first-team All-American. He was the No. 1 overall pick by the Pittsburgh Steelers and won the NFL rushing title twice. He was a two-time Pro Bowler and had an eleven-year career with the Steelers, Detroit Lions, and Washington Redskins.

Shawn Moore/Herman Moore

The Moores were not related. But in 1990, they made sure the blood ran through the Virginia football team's offense. Quarterback Shawn Moore and wide receiver Herman Moore directed Virginia to a 7-0 start their senior season, and the Cavaliers were ranked No. 1 in the country the last three weeks of that run. In week eight, the Moores were again swift and powerful, but Georgia Tech won the offensive battle 41-38, and the Yellow Jackets went on to finish undefeated and earn a share of the national title with Colorado. Shawn Moore dislocated his thumb when it was stepped on at Maryland, and the Cavaliers went on to finish 8-4 even though the quarterback returned for a nail-biting 23-22 loss to Tennessee in the Sugar Bowl. Shawn Moore finished fourth in the Heisman Trophy voting and Herman Moore sixth. Herman was drafted in the first round by the Detroit Lions and went on to have a long, fruitful NFL career. Shawn went in the eleventh round to the Denver Broncos, lasting three seasons primarily as a backup. He returned to UVa as part of Mike London's coaching staff.

ARENA

John Paul Jones Arena: John Paul Jones Arena opened in 2006, providing the Cavaliers men's and women's basketball teams a home with a seating capacity of 14,593, nearly double that of the aging University Hall that it replaced. It is named after a 1948 graduate of UVa Law who donated $20 million to get the push for a new arena started in 2001. Five years later, his son, 1976 UVa grad Paul Tudor Jones, donated $35 million for naming rights and requested the honor go to his father. The arena features pergolas, to tie into the design of Scott Stadium. The Cavaliers notched two big wins in the new home in 2007, beating Duke for the first time in five seasons, then defeating Virginia Tech to clinch a share of the ACC regular-season title.

NOTABLE ALUMS

Robert F. Kennedy and Edward Kennedy
U.S. senators and presidential candidates

Samuel Goldwyn
President MGM

Walter Reed
Medical pioneer who discovered vaccine for Yellow Fever

Katie Couric
TV news anchor

Tina Fey
Actress

STADIUM

Scott Stadium: Scott Stadium opened in 1931, named after UVa rector Frederic Scott. It held 25,000 and offered a picturesque view of the Blue Ridge Mountains, particularly Monticello Mountain, through the open end of the stadium. Scott has gone through several expansions, as well as transitions to artificial turf and then back to natural grass. The biggest crowd at Scott was 64,947, which saw Virginia fall 52-7 to USC in 2008. One of the most notable ACC games at Scott came on a Thursday night in November 1995, when the Cavaliers became the first ACC team to beat Florida State in a conference game, ending the Seminoles' twenty-nine-game league winning streak.

CUSE CONNECTION

ALL-TIME FOOTBALL RECORD VS. SYRACUSE: 2-2

1975: Syracuse 37, Virginia 0

1977: Syracuse 6, Virginia 3

2004: Virginia 31, Syracuse 10

2005: Virginia 27, Syracuse 24

ALL-TIME BASKETBALL RECORD VS. SYRACUSE: 1-3

1984: Virginia 63, Syracuse 55

1990: Syracuse 63, Virginia 61 (NCAA Tournament)

2007: Syracuse 70, Virginia 68

2008: Syracuse 73, Virginia 70

Comeback spoiled: On September 27, 2005, in the Carrier Dome, Syracuse trailed 25th-ranked Virginia 24-14 entering the fourth quarter. Led by quarterback Perry Patterson and tight end Joe Kowalewski, the Orange fought back to tie it at twenty-four. The Cavaliers deflated the dome fans with one final drive. Coach Al Groh elected to go for a fourth-and-one at the SU nine to run the clock, and fullback Jason Snelling picked up four yards. Then Connor Hughes kicked a nineteen-yard field goal as time expired to lift Virginia to a 27-24 victory. Patterson ran for two TDs and Kowalewski caught seven passes in defeat.

Big NCAA block by DC: The mood was tense on March 18, 1990, in the Richmond Coliseum as Billy Owens stepped to the free-throw line with fourteen seconds left and Syracuse leading Virginia by two. Owens missed the front end of a one-and-one, Virginia rebounded, and John Crotty took the ball upcourt looking to win with a three or tie. Kenny Turner passed up a trey in the corner to feed Bryant Stith. But Derrick Coleman blocked Stith's shot to preserve SU's 63-61 win and propel the Orange to the Sweet 16.

Big Rick in relief: Syracuse trailed by as many as thirteen points on November 28, 2008, in the Carrier Dome, and some fans worried it was a hangover from beating ranked Florida and home-team Kansas two nights in a row to win the championship of the CBE Classic. Center Arinze Onuako was held scoreless in the first half and picked up foul No. 4 early in the second. But Rick Jackson came in as a super sub with eight points and six rebounds as Syracuse came back to win 73-70. Jonny Flynn and Andy Rautins led the way with fifteen points each and SU remained unbeaten.

MASCOT

The UVa mascot is the Cavalier. Tradition had the Cavalier ride into football games on a horse, but this came to a halt in 1974 when artificial turf was installed at Scott Stadium. In the 1989 Citrus Bowl the rider and horse made a comeback, and it was so acclaimed they returned to Scott Stadium the following season. The costumed mascot who plays on the sidelines is called CavMan. The horse he rides in on is named Sabre.

"The Good Old Song"

The good old song of Wahoo Wah!

We'll sing it o'er and o'er!

It cheers our hearts and warms our blood

To hear the shout and roar

We come from old Vir-Gin-I-A

Where all is bright and gay

Let's all join hands and give a yell

For good old U-V-A!

OTHER SPORTS

The Syracuse men's lacrosse team has a ready-made ACC rivalry set up with the squad from Virginia. The Cavaliers have won seven national championships, two in the days before the NCAA Tournament era, in 1952 and 1970, and five in the tournament, in 1972, 1999, 2003, 2006, and 2011. The Orange and Cavaliers have often tangled in the regular season, most times with the No. 1 ranking at stake. They've played every season since 1994, and either Syracuse or Virginia has won ten of the eighteen national titles since then.

GAME DAY

MEDIA

Broadcasting the Game: WINA 1070 AM and WWWV 97.5 FM, Charlottesville

Covering the Cavaliers: www.dailyprogress.com (*Charlottesville Daily Progress*), www.dailypress.com (*Hampton Daily Press*), www.cavaliersdaily.com (UVa student newspaper), espn.go.com/blog/ACC/post (ESPN ACC blog), www.thesabre.com (website devoted to UVa sports)

TAILGATING

The UVa sports site says, "Tailgating is a longstanding tradition at the University of Virginia." It's allowed at all university lots designated for event parking. These lots open at 8 a.m. and remain open until midnight. Charcoal grills are not allowed. Propane grills are limited to tanks of five pounds or less. Alcohol is permitted but must be kept in designated areas. The general public can park in lots on the North Grounds and Fontaine Research Park for free, first-come, first-served. The general public can also park in garages at Emmet Street and Ivy Road, Central Grounds, UVa Health System area, and downtown Charlottesville. The garage fee is $10 for football games and $5 for basketball games. For information, go to www.virginia.edu/parking/events.

SHUTTLE

A shuttle service is run by the Charlottesville Pupil Transportation, with stops at Market and Water streets. The shuttles are not handicapped accessible. State-issued handicapped placards are needed to park in the North Grounds area. Shuttles from there are handicapped accessible. For more shuttle information go to www.virginiasports.com/parking.

TRADITIONS

"Guys in ties, girls in pearls": The attire of choice for students at Scott Stadium was dress shirts and ties for the men and sundresses for the women. During the tenure of Head Coach Al Groh, though, more students began dressing in orange T-shirts at his request. Alumni, however, tended to stick to the motto "guys in ties, girls in pearls."

Battle on "Hoo Vision": Just before the start of every home football game, an animated feature displayed on the big screen called "Hoo Vision" gets the crowd going. CavMan is always shown in a recognizable campus spot, vanquishing the mascot of the opposing team.

ABOUT TOWN

Charlottesville predates the birth of the nation. It was founded in 1762 and has played a role in the lives of subsequent U.S. presidents Thomas Jefferson, James Monroe, and James Madison. Jefferson was the father of UVa. His home, Monticello, is a popular Charlottesville visitors destination. Charlottesville sits in the geographic center of Virginia, along the Rivanna River and parallel to the Blue Ridge Mountains. It has a population of 43,375. Albemarle County surrounds the city, bringing the area's total population to 118,398.

LODGING

Boar's Head Inn: This resort-like hotel is owned by UVa and proudly declares itself as the official hotel of the University of Virginia. The inn's property includes a golf course, tennis courts, pool, and spa. It sits beside a lake. There's a nineteenth-century gristmill that's been rebuilt. And there's the 1834 Pub, too. *200 Ednam Dr., Charlottesville, VA 22903, 434-296-2181, www. boarsheadinn.com*

Hampton Inn & Suites Charlottesville at the University: The chain hotel with free breakfast has hit the jackpot in location and pretty setting in Charlottesville. This Hampton is in the middle of the bricked-street center of shopping and dining. *900 W. Main St., Charlottesville, VA 22903, 434-923-8600, www.hamptoninn3/en/hotels/virginia/hampton-inn-and-suites-charlottesville*

Cavalier Inn: This is a five-story, steel-and-glass motel that's just a half-mile west of UVa's famed Rotunda. It's also owned by the University of Virginia and is close to both Scott Stadium and John Paul Jones Arena. *105 N. Emmet St., Charlottesville, VA 22903, 888-882-2129, www.cavalierinn.com*

EATING

The College Inn: Since 1950, UVa students who wanted to grab a slice have headed to The Corner and stopped at the College Inn. That's a lot of pizza in Cavalier tummies. The interior has been renovated, but traditional values— pizzas, sandwiches, pasta, and Greek and Italian favorites—remain. *1511 University Ave., Charlottesville, VA 22903, 434-977-2710, www.thecollegeinn.com*

The Continental Divide: This is the favorite little Charlottesville spot for Mexican food and margaritas. A neon sign urges "Get in here." If you listen, you'll be treated to fish or pork tacos, sushi-grade tuna, and red-hot blues music. *811 W. Main St., Charlottesville, VA 22903, 434-984-0143*

Littlejohn's New York Deli: In 1976, heads were put together to declare that students coming from up North needed some comfort food. They slice meat and cheese on-site daily to meet those needs. Special sandwiches include the Wild Turkey, Five Easy Pieces, Nuclear Sub, and Ranch Hand, all from the minds of UVa students that worked the kitchen at Littlejohn's. *1427 Varsity Ave., Charlottesville, VA 22903, 434-977-0588, www.littlejohnsdeli.com*

SIGHTSEEING

Stroll The Grounds: That is with a capital T and G. Since the days of Thomas Jefferson, everybody associated with the University of Virginia calls the campus The Grounds. The architecture is beautiful, from the Rome-inspired Rotuda to the bricks that surround The Lawn. Yes, there is an official tour to point out the highlights. *www.virginia.edu/uvatours/groundstour*

Monticello: Visiting Monticello is like a time travel back to the days of Thomas Jefferson. In fact, over 90 percent of the mansion that sits on Jefferson's beloved plot of land is the original. Visitors are allowed to explore the first floor of the house, as well as the lawn and gardens. *931 Thomas Jefferson Parkway, Charlottesville, VA 22902, 434-984-9800, www.monticello.org*

SHOPPING

Mincer's: The family owned operation in The Corner started as a tobacco store in 1948. The Mincers proved to be diligent and nimble. As interest in smoking decreased, the store cut the Humidor portion of its name out altogether to concentrate on clothing and accessories with the UVa imprint. There's T-shirts galore and way more. *1527 University Ave., Charlottesville, VA 22903, 434-296-5687, www.mincers.com*

Antiques in a new light: The owners of Circa call it an affordable antiques store. Plenty of UVa students take them up on that pledge to put the final touches on the dorm room or apartment. But the town portion of town-and-gown is into Circa, too. They declare that they turn over their inventory so quickly that it would take too long to put individual pieces up on their website. And still the 10,000 square-foot store is full of cool stuff and open for browsing. *1700 Allied St., Charlottesville, VA 22903, 434-295-5760, www.circainc.com*

NIGHTLIFE

Miller's Downtown: This pub offers plenty more than its namesake beer. In addition to brew and drink specials, Miller's has lasted thirty years by featuring good bar food, an outdoor patio voted best-of in local contests, and a third-floor billiards room (or pool tables, if that's more your cue). *101 W. Main St., Charlottesville, VA 22902, 434-971-8511, millersdowntown.com*

Beer Run: Can UVa students buy kegs at Beer Run? You betcha. But this popular spot also features the Buffalo Burger, Bloody Marys, and Natty Bo's (that's National Bohemian to those of you who've never been lucky enough to order one in the brewery's hometown of Baltimore). *156 Carlton Rd., Charlottesville, VA 22902, 434-984-2337, www.beerrun.com*

Positively Fourth Street: One of the newest servers of food and drink in Charlottesville quickly began lighting up the rating boards at yelp and urbanspoon. Folks like their burgers, wine choices, and—shades of a couple states south—their mint juleps. As Bobby Dylan himself loves to sing, gotta serve somebody. *401 E. Main St., Charlottesville, VA 22902, 434-974-9464, positively4thst.com*

LAST-MINUTE TIPS

Where to Shop: The place to hang for UVa students, faculty, and staff since the 1890s is called The Corner. It's a strip of bars, boutiques, and restaurants that borders the campus from 12 1/2 Street SW to Chancellor Street.

Where to Buy Tickets: Folks generally hold up tickets for sale around The Corner. You can also hunt on the University of Virginia page on stubhub.com. There's a ticket exchange board on www.thesabre.com that prohibits selling tickets for more than face value.

TRAVELING TO CHARLOTTESVILLE?

Charlottesville is about a ten-mile drive from the Charlottesville-Abermarle Airport. It is about a two-hour drive southwest from Washington, D.C.

Virginia Tech

VIRGINIA POLYTECHNIC INSTITUTE AND STATE UNIVERSITY

STUDENTS
28,830

BLACKSBURG
pop. 42,620

LANE STADIUM
65,632

CASSELL COLISEUM
10,052

COLORS
Chicago Maroon &
Burnt Orange

NICKNAME
Hokies

MASCOT
HokieBird

CAMPUS ATTRACTIONS
Victims Memorial,
Torgersen Hall Bridge,
Hahn Horticulture Garden

PHONE
540-231-6596
(general information)

540-231-6411
(campus police)

540-231-6796
(athletic department)

TICKETS
800-828-3244 or
www.hokiesports.com

In 1872, the Virginia General Assembly purchased the facilities of Preston and Olin Institute, a small Methodist college, and founded Virginia Agricultural and Mechanical College.

Included in the studies was a military component. In fact, until 1932, every physically able male student had to serve four years in the Corps of Cadets. That year the requirement was changed to two years of service. In 1964, serving in the Corps of Cadets became voluntary. Today, about one thousand students still serve in the Corps of Cadets, and the Virginia Tech motto remains *Ut Prosium*, which translates to That I May Serve.

In 1944, the college officially changed its name to Virginia Polytechnic Institute. For decades, that was usually shorted in the sports pages to VPI. In 1970, school officials added "and State University" to the name, and the nickname morphed to the sleeker Virginia Tech.

The world will always recall the tragic day of April 16, 2007, when Virginia Tech student Seung-Hui Cho killed thirty-two and wounded seventeen others during two separate shooting incidents before taking his own life.

What has become known as the Virginia Tech Massacre forever changed lives in Blacksburg. Friends and family remembered those slain, and everybody struggled to reconcile how it could have happened and drew plans to make sure it would never again. A campus tribute to those slain, known as the Victims Memorial, features thirty-two large stones, each holding the name of somebody who lost their life in the tragedy.

The Virginia Tech football team has had several chapters of success before the reign of current coach Frank Beamer, whose twenty-six years as head coach at his alma mater has secured an overall record of 216-104-2 and frequent success in first the Big East since 1991, and then in the ACC since 2004. Beamer led Virginia Tech to its most successful season, going 11-0 in 1999 before falling short of a national title by losing to Florida State 46-25 in the 2000 Sugar Bowl.

Virginia Tech has been playing football since 1897. The school's first bowl trip was to the 1947 Sun Bowl. The Hokies lost 18-16 to Cincinnati. Virginia Tech has played in a bowl game twenty consecutive seasons, the third longest streak in the nation, behind only Florida State and Florida.

Three stalwart coaches led Virginia Tech to winning records as an independent: Frank Moseley, from 1951 to 1960; Jerry Claiborne, from 1961 to 1970; and Bill Dooley, from 1978 to 1986.

Virginia Tech started playing basketball in January 1909. In fact, the second season on the court, 1909-10, remains the school's only undefeated season with a record of 11-0.

Charles Moir had the most success, directing Virginia Tech to an overall record of 213-119 from 1976 to 1987. The coach that proceded him, Don DeVoe, is considered a Hokies legend for his mark of 88-45 from 1976 to 1987. Bill Foster went 101-78 from 1991 to 1997, which included Virginia Tech's winningest season, 25-10, in 1994-95. James Johnson took over from Seth Greenberg before last season. Greenberg's teams went 170-123 from 2003 to 2012 but only made the NCAA Tournament once.

The Hokies' biggest tournament successes have come in the NIT, of which they won the championship twice, in 1973 and 1995. The best Virginia Tech has done in the NCAA Tournament is two victories, in 1967.

Football

NATIONAL CHAMPIONSHIPS (0): The Hokies lost to Florida State, 46-25, in the 2000 Sugar Bowl, to finish 11-1.

ACC CHAMPIONSHIPS (0):

BOWL RECORD: 10-15 (.400). Last bowl—13-10 over Rutgers in 2012 Russell Athletic Bowl

LONGEST WINNING STREAK: 13 games, 1995-96

WINNINGEST COACH: Frank Beamer (1987-present), 216-104-2 (.671)

HEISMAN TROPHY WINNERS OR HIGHEST HEISMAN FINISH:
Quarterback Michael Vick, third, 1990

Basketball

NATIONAL CHAMPIONSHIPS (0): The Hokies won two games to reach the Elite Eight in the 1967 NCAA Tournament.

ACC CHAMPIONSHIPS (0): The Hokies' best mark in the ACC is 10-6, in 2006-07 and 2009-10.

NCAA TOURNAMENT RECORD: 6-8 (.429) Last appearance—Lost 63-48 to Southern Illinois in the second round of the 2007 tournament.

WINNINGEST COACH: Charles Moir (1976-87), 213-119 (.659)

NATIONAL PLAYERS OF THE YEAR (0):

LEGENDS

Michael Vick

Quarterback Vick mesmerized the college football world with his arm and his legs for two seasons before setting off to do the same with the Atlanta Falcons and then Philadelphia Eagles of the NFL. As a freshman in 1999, Vick led the Hokies to a perfect 11-0 regular-season record before Virginia Tech lost to Florida State in an offensive shootout in the game for the national championship in the Sugar Bowl. After the season, Vick won the ESPY from ESPN for College Football Player of the Year. Vick also was a first-team All-American after completing 59.2 percent for 1,840 yards and 12 TDs while running for 585 yards and eight TDs. Vick's No. 7 jersey was retired in 2002.

Bruce Smith

Before he became the favorite sack man for the Buffalo Bills, Smith was the king of the defensive line at Virginia Tech. Smith won the Outland Trophy given to the nation's top lineman after his senior season in 1984. Smith was a big guy for nailing the carrier behind the line of scrimmage. He accounted for 71 tackles for a total of 504 yards lost in his four years and was a consensus All-American his senior year, too. Smith's No. 78 is one of four numbers retired by the Hokies.

Corey Moore

Corey Moore took home two national awards after his senior season in 1999, the Bronko Nagurski Award for best defensive player of the year and the Lombardi Award for lineman of the year. He also became the first man in the Big East to win back-to-back conference defensive player of the year awards. In three seasons at Virginia Tech, Moore was credited with thirty-five sacks. He was drafted in the second round by the Buffalo Bills. Virginia Tech retired his No. 56 jersey in 2009.

Dell Curry

Guard Curry was on four straight Virginia Tech teams—from 1983 to 1986—that made either the NCAA or NIT tournament. He led the Metro Conference in scoring his senior year with an average of 24.1 points, and the Hokies retired his jersey in a ceremony before his last home game. His 2,389 career points was the most in school history at the time. Curry's three-point-shooting prowess lifted him to a fifteen-season career in the NBA. He retired with a career three-point percentage of forty.

Vernell "Bimbo" Coles

Guard Coles knew how to put the biscuit in the basket. He finished his Virginia Tech career as the leading scorer in the history of the school and the Metro Conference. The Hokies retired his No. 12 jersey before his last home game in 1990. While in college, Coles made the U.S. Olympic Team in 1988 and helped lead the team to a bronze medal at the Seoul Games. Coles played in the NBA from 1990 to 2004, with five different teams.

ARENA

Cassell Coliseum: Virginia Tech's basketball arena was completed in 1964 with the name of Student Activities and Physical Education Building. But it held its first basketball game in 1962, while still under construction. The name was changed to Cassell Coliseum in 1976 to honor Stuart K. Cassell, a 1932 alumnus who became a professor, chief business officer, and vice president of administration at Virginia Tech. The arena was expanded twice, in 1984 and 1998, but remains known for its distinctive laminated wood arches. Although capacity is listed at 10,052, Virginia Tech squeezed 11,500 into the arena for a game against Purdue in 1966.

NOTABLE ALUMS

Sharyn E. McCrumb
Novelist of Appalachian culture–themed books

Homer Hikam
Writer whose *Rocket Boys* was turned into movie *October Sky*

Roger Craig
Winner of 2011 *Jeopardy!* tournament of champions

Hoda Kotb
Today TV anchor

Roger K. Crouch
Scientific astronaut on *Space Shuttle Columbia*

STADIUM

Lane Stadium: Lane Stadium is named after Edward Hudson Lane Sr., who attended the school in the early 1900s and went on to found the Lane Company, the world's most-renowned maker of cedar chests, and join the school's board of visitors. Lane Stadium opened in 1965 with a capacity of 35,000. A handful of expansion projects have brought it to what it is today: a big, rowdy stadium with a reputation as one of the toughest places to play on the road in the nation.

OTHER SPORTS

The Virginia Tech track and field squad has a number of individual NCAA champions to its credit. In 2012 the men's team had an indoor and outdoor NCAA champion in a field event. Marcell Lomnicky was No. 1 in the weight throw at the indoor championships, and Alexander Ziegler took the title in the hammer throw at the outdoor championships. On the women's side, hurdler Queen Harrison won the NCAA title at 60 meters in the 2010 indoor championships and two crowns, in the 100 and 400, at the outdoor championships.

CUSE CONNECTION

ALL-TIME FOOTBALL RECORD VS. SYRACUSE: 8-9

Last meeting October 11, 2003: Virginia Tech 51, Syracuse 7

ALL-TIME BASKETBALL RECORD VS. SYRACUSE: 2-4

Last meeting November 23, 2011: Syracuse 69, Virginia Tech 58

Donovan's a dilly: Virginia Tech scored with its feared special teams by returning a blocked punt for a touchdown. The Hokies scored in a rare way, intercepting a two-point try pass and taking it the distance for their own two points instead. But on November 14, 1988, in the Carrier Dome, Orange star quarterback Donovan McNabb had the final say with his arm and his legs. McNabb either passed or ran himself on twelve of the fourteen plays of a final drive that ended with Syracuse scoring a game-winning touchdown on a play that it seems the Orange patented. McNabb rolled to his right and then threw to tight end Stephen Brominski on the left side to give Syracuse the 28-26 victory.

Taking down No. 8: Virginia Tech was 8-1 and ranked No. 8 in the country and Syracuse was just 3-6 on November 9, 2002, in the Carrier Dome, but the Orange came away with a 50-42 win in three overtimes. SU running back Damien Rhodes scored on a twenty-five-yard run and then ran in the two-point conversion in the third overtime. On the next play, Syracuse safety Maurice McClain intercepted Bryan Randall's pass, and the game was over. Walter Reyes rushed for 118 yards for the Orange, and quarterback Troy Nunes passed for 403 yards.

Early Garden Party: Syracuse Athletic Director Daryl Gross has branded the Orange as New York's college team. The Syracuse basketball team indeed plays at the famed Madison Square Garden with a swagger. On November 23, 2011, Syracuse took to the Big Apple and its basketball mecca to face Virginia Tech in the semifinals of the Preseason NIT. Kris Joseph scored twenty points and gathered ten rebounds, and Brandon Triche added eighteen points and six assists to turn back the Hokies. Jarrell Eddie had eighteen points to lead the Hokies, who fell to 3-1 as Syracuse improved to 5-0.

"Tech Triumph"

Techmen, we're Techmen, with spirit true and faithful
Backing up our team with hopes undying
Techmen, oh, Techmen, we're out to win today
Showing pep and life to which we're trying
V.P., old V.P., you know our hearts are with you
In our luck which never seems to die
Win or lose we'll greet you with a glad returning
You're the pride of V.P.I.

Just watch our men so big and active
Support the Orange and Maroon
Let's go Techs! We know our ends and backs are stronger
With winning hopes, we fear defeat no longer
To see our team plow through the line, boys
Determined now to win or die
So give a Hokie, Hokie, Hokie, Hi
Rae, Ri, Old V.P.I.

Fight men, oh, fight men! We're going to be champions
Adding to our list another victory
Football or baseball, the games in which we star
They're the sports that made old V.P. famous
Hold them, just hold them! You know the corps is behind you
Watching every movement that you make
Winning games was nothing for our teams before us
Keep the "rep" for V.P.'s sake

GAME DAY

MEDIA

Broadcasting the Game: WBRW-FM 105.3 in Blacksburg

Covering the Hokies: www.roanoke.com (*Roanoke Times*), www.timesdispatch.com (*Richmond Times Dispatch*), www.dailypress.com (*Hampton Roads Daily Press*), www.collegiatetimes.com (Virginia Tech student newspaper), espn.go.com/blog/ACC (ESPN ACC blog)

TAILGATING

Tailgating is allowed but must be confined to the area immediately behind your vehicle. Do not block sidewalks. Do not throw any objects. Do not hook up sound systems. Tailgaters consuming alcohol can expect to be asked for ID. Public parking is available at designated campus lots. Parking is on a first-come, first-served basis. The fee is $15, For information, go to www.hokiesports.com/football/fanguide.

SHUTTLE

Additional public parking is available in the lots outside Old Blacksburg High School, 520 Patrick Henry Blvd., for a fee of $8, and Blacksburg High School, 3109 Prices Fork Rd., for a fee of $12. A shuttle service is provided from both sites as part of the fee. Shuttle starts three hours before game time. For information, go to www.hokiesports.com/football/fanguide/parking.

MASCOT

The HokieBird that roams the sidelines today started off as the Gobbler, and then the Fighting Gobbler. Yes, Virginia Tech has an alternate nickname. There are contrasting tales of how the Gobblers came about. One has several cadets returning in 1907 from a Thanksgiving Day football game vs. North Carolina and proclaiming that VPI "took the turkey." Another gives bearing to the fact that athletes were known to "gobble their food." In any case, a costumed Gobbler took the field in 1936.

In 1981, a mascot in the new design for the costume was delivered to the football field by helicopter before a game against Wake Forest. The name HokieBird stuck from then on.

TRADITIONS

Enter Sandman: In 2000, Virginia Tech officials started using the classic heavy metal song "Enter Sandman" as the football squad's entrance cue into Lane Stadium. The place rocks as every fan jumps up and down. You can't escape the shake, rattle, and rock 'n roll.

Smoked Turkey Legs: Fans can see and smell the Gobblers portion of the Virginia Tech tradition right inside Lane Stadium. One of the food offerings at the concession stands is smoked turkey legs. They say that 1,500 of them are bought and eaten in the seats every home game. Take a good whiff.

TECHMEN
WE ARE
TECHMEN

ABOUT TOWN

Blacksburg was founded in 1798 by the sons of settler Samuel Black. It's the largest town in Virginia, with a population of 42,620. Along with neighboring Christiansburg and Radford, it's part of a metropolitan statistical area of 159,587. In 2011, *Businessweek* called Blacksburg the best place in the United States to raise children, and *Southern Living* cited it as the best college town in the South.

LODGING

The Inn at Virginia Tech and Skelton Conference Center: The Inn at Virginia Tech is not only the sole on-campus hotel, it's also the biggest hotel in Blacksburg. It was built in 2005, with its distinctive look coming from 2,741 tons of HokieStone. The complex is home to two eateries: Preston's Restaurant and the more informal Continental Divide Lounge. *901 Prices Fork Rd., Blacksburg, VA 24061, 540-231-8000, www.innatvirginiatech.com*

Main Street Inn: Rip McGinnis kept his years at Virginia Tech so close to his heart that the Virginia Beach Realty and Development Company owner decided to open this thirty-four-suite hotel in Blacksburg. His wife, Darlene, did much of the decorating. They've put together a fine hotel that's walking distance to Lane Stadium and Cassell Coliseum. And they love to point guests toward the other attractions in this home away from home, their beloved New River Valley. *205 S. Main St., Blacksburg, VA 24060, 540-552-6246, www.hotelblacksburg.com*

EATING

The Cellar Restaurant: The Cellar has been feeding Blacksburg since 1963 with food, beer, and local music. The menu includes Chesapeake Bay crab cakes as well as pizza and pasta. The music stand can present Irish one night, Americana the next, and jazz the third. *301 N. Main St., Blacksburg, VA 24060, 540-953-0651, www.the-cellar.com*

Gillies: Jan Gillie opened the place as an ice cream stand in 1974. A year later, it became one of Blacksburg's first restaurants to specialize in soup and bread. In the 1980s, Ranae Gillie joined the operation. Now the restaurant is known for its "vibrant and welcoming atmosphere" featuring progressive vegetarian fare and seafood. *153 College Ave., Blacksburg, VA 24060, 540-961-2703, www. gilliesrestaurant.net*

Cabo Fish Taco and Baja Seagrill: The restaurant is owned by a trio of Virginia Tech graduates. Chef Rob Crenshaw and numbers guy Gary Walker were surfers from Virginia Beach. Rob's wife, Maeghan Crenshaw, is the designer of the restaurant's unique style. How cool? The Food Network's Guy Fieri was there to spread the word about the fish tacos and way more. *117 S. Main St., Blacksburg, VA 24060, 540-552-0950, www.cabofishtaco.com*

SIGHTSEEING

Hahn Horticulture Garden: The Hahn Horticulture Garden was founded in 1984 as a way to teach students and community members about plant material, landscaping, and environmental awareness. It was named the Hahn Horticulture Garden in 2004 in honor to Peggy Lee Hahn, a contributor and terrific gardener in her own right. The six-acre, on-campus grounds feature plants from around the world, in shade gardens, water gardens, and an indoor pavilion. *540-231-5970, www.hort.vt.edu/hhg*

The Lyric Theatre: Since 1998, the Lyric has been operating as a not-for-profit theater and community center. They invite movie and old theater lovers alike to eat popcorn, relish the restored tapestries of the 1930s, and soak in the historic and hip vibe. It features live events as well as movies. *135 College Ave., Blacksburg, VA 24060, 540-951-0604, www.thelyric.com*

SHOPPING

The T-Shirt Factory: This is the place to shop if you want to pick up souvenirs that tell folks back home that you've been to Blacksburg, and you're too much of a Syracuse Orange fan to wear anything with a Virginia Tech emblem, logo, or saying on it. The T-Shirt Factory favors material from the state of Virginia and the Blue Ridge Mountains as well as Virginia Tech gear. *209 College Ave., Blacksburg, VA 24060, 540-953-1293, www.discoverourtown.com/VA/Blacksburg*

New River Valley Mall: If you'd like to get out of town for a shopping trip, the New River Valley Mall is in neighboring Christiansburg, just 4 1/2 miles to the southeast. There's a Dick's Sporting Goods, a Sears, and a JC Penney. If you'd like to visit a department store that's not yet in Central New York, Belk is one of the anchors, too. *782 New River Rd., Christiansburg, VA 24073, 540-382-4927, www.shopnewrivervalleymall.com*

NIGHTLIFE

Sharkey's Wing and Rib Joint: Every page you click on as you navigate Sharkey's website features a pair of frosty mugs full of draft beers. At the bar, you see, there are plenty of domestic favorites, including a handful with regional flair. Doesn't a Breckenridge Vanilla Porter sound good right now? Ah, go ahead, grab a Yuengling and watch the big-screen TVs that make Sharkey's a top sports bar. Order a burger or the signature wings or ribs. *220 N. Main St., Blacksburg, VA 24060, 540-552-2030, www.sharkeyswingandribjoint.com*

Big Al's Grille & Sports Bar: Big Al's opens at 10 a.m. on football game days. 'Nuff said. OK, there's plenty of bar food fare from the grille and plenty of variety at the bar. The TVs will feature the Hokies. *201 N. Main St., Blacksburg, VA 24060, 540-951-3300, www.bigalssportsbar.com*

LAST-MINUTE TIPS

Where to Shop: You can't go wrong on Main Street in a college town on game day. In Blacksburg, you can find the Tech Bookstore as well as the Campus Emporium on South Main. They both provide plenty of Hokies Chicago Maroon & Burnt Orange clothing and more to peruse and perhaps purchase.

Where to Buy Tickets: Games at Lane Stadium and Cassell Coliseum can both be tough tickets. Students have to get their tickets through a lottery and are not supposed to sell them. That only makes the game-day hawkers work with a sharper edge. And there's always stubhub.com.

Bull & Bones Brewhaus and Grill: The hand-crafted beer and ale brews in the middle of the fine restaurant and sports bar. The bar features championship billiards tables and other interactive games for the sports fan who needs to fit a little bit of do into their watching schedule. *1470 S. Main St., Blacksburg, VA 24060, 540-953-2855, www.bullandbones.com*

TRAVELING TO BLACKSBURG?

Blacksburg is about a fifty-minute drive from Roanoke Regional Airport. The two nearest major airports, Richmond International and Charlotte Douglas, are both about three hours away, Charlotte about 2 hours, 45 minutes and Richmond about 3 hours, 15 minutes. A drive from Syracuse to Blacksburg would take almost nine hours.

Wake Forest

Wake Forest was chartered in 1830 by the Baptist State Convention of North Carolina. One of the school's early leaders was Samuel Wait, a graduate of Columbia College in New York who was appointed by the convention to canvass the state and explain to churches and individuals the need for a college. He traveled the state between 1830 and 1832. The school's original name was the Wake Forest Manual Labor Institute, and it was located in Wake Forest, North Carolina. Wait's home is now a historical museum in the town of Wake Forest.

Sixteen students registered when Wake Forest first opened its doors in 1834. Wait had been elected principal. Within a year, enrollment had increased to more than seventy students.

In 1838, the school's name was changed to Wake Forest College. In 1854, Washington Manly Wingate, a twenty-six-year-old graduate of Wake Forest, was chosen as the first alumnus to serve as the school's president.

Wake Forest College suspended classes for three years during the Civil War. During the war, the school's buildings were used for a girls school and, later, a military hospital

WAKE FOREST UNIVERSITY

STUDENTS
4,657

WINSTON-SALEM
pop. 232,385

BB&T FIELD
31,500

LAWRENCE JOEL VETERANS MEMORIAL COLISEUM
14,665

COLORS
Old Gold and Black

NICKNAME
Demon Deacons

MASCOT
Deacon

CAMPUS ATTRACTIONS
Wait Chapel,
Z. Smith Reynolds Library

PHONE
336-758-5000
(general information)

336-758-5911
(campus police)

336-758-5616
(athletic department)

TICKETS
888-758-DEAC or
www.WakeForestSports.com

for the Confederate government. In 1865, despite an endowment that had shrunk from nearly $100,000 prior to the war to just $11,000, Wake Forest re-opened.

In 1875, a Wake Forest student named James Denmark convinced the state legislature to charter the North Carolina Baptist Student Loan Fund. It was the first college student loan fund in the United States, and it's known today as the James W. Denmark Loan Fund. By 1902, the School of Law and the School of Medicine had been founded. In 1941, the School of Medicine was relocated to Winston-Salem. It's now known as the Bowman Gray School of Medicine. In 1942, women were admitted to the college.

In 1946, the Z. Smith Reynolds Foundation proposed that up to $350,000 a year of the income from the foundation be given in perpetuity to Wake Forest College, provided the entire college was relocated to Winston-Salem. The Board of Trustees and the Baptist Convention both accepted. During ground-breaking ceremonies in 1951, President Harry S. Truman scooped the first shovel of dirt at the new campus. Wake Forest opened in Winston-Salem in the summer of 1956. And in 1967, Wake Forest became a university. The old campus in Wake Forest is now the home of the Southeastern Baptist Theological Seminary.

Wake Forest played the first intercollegiate basketball game held in the state of North Carolina. In 1906, Wake Forest defeated Trinity, which is now Duke, 15-5 at Angier Duke Gymnasium. In 1936, Wake Forest joined the Southern Conference, and in 1939 Wake Forest was one of eight teams to play in the first NCAA Tournament. On its original campus Wake Forest played in Gore Gymnasium, a 2,200-seat facility. From 1958 to 1966, Bones McKinney guided Wake Forest to two ACC titles and the 1962 Final Four during his eight years as coach. Wake Forest's history is full of notable players from Len Chappell and Billy Packer to Tim Duncan and Chris Paul.

Wake Forest's football program dates back to 1888. In the only game that season, Wake Forest defeated North Carolina 6-4 on October 18, 1888. Wake Forest played in its first bowl game in 1946, defeating South Carolina 26-14 in the inaugural Gator Bowl. Wake Forest was coached by Peahead Walker. Bill Barnes was Wake Forest's first ACC player of the year, and in 1964, the legendary Brian Piccolo received the honor. Chris Barclay led the ACC in rushing three times, including 2005 when he was named ACC player of the year.

Football

NATIONAL CHAMPIONSHIPS (0): Wake Forest finished the 2006 season ranked 15th in the country.

ACC CHAMPIONSHIPS (2): 1970, 2006

BOWL RECORD: 6-3 (.667). Last bowl—23-17 loss to Mississippi State in the 2011 Music City Bowl

LONGEST WINNING STREAK: 7 games (1944). Wake Forest won the first seven games of the 1944 season. After a loss to Duke, Wake Forest ended the season with a win over South Carolina to finish with an 8-1 record.

WINNINGEST COACH: D.C. Walker (1937-50), 77-51-6 (.597)

HEISMAN TROPHY WINNERS OR HIGHEST HEISMAN FINISH: Running back Brian Piccolo, 10th in 1964

Basketball

NATIONAL CHAMPIONSHIPS (0): Wake Forest lost to Ohio State in the 1962 Final Four. The Demon Deacons beat UCLA in the consolation game.

ACC CHAMPIONSHIPS (4): 1961, 1962, 1995, 1996; 4 regular-season championships: 1960, 1962, 1995, 2003

NCAA TOURNAMENT RECORD: 23-16 (.589). Last NCAA appearance—75-66 loss to Ohio State in the second round of the 2010 tournament.

WINNINGEST COACH: Murray Greason (1934-57), 288-244 (.541)

NATIONAL PLAYERS OF THE YEAR: Tim Duncan in 1997

LEGENDS

Brian Piccolo

Piccolo played at Wake Forest from 1962 to 1964. As a senior, Piccolo set ACC records for carries (252) and yards gained (1,044). He led the country with 111 points. He was named the ACC Player of the Year and earned All-America honors. He wasn't drafted but still spent five years with the Chicago Bears. He died of cancer in 1970 at the age of twenty-six. His battle with cancer and his friendship with Bears great Gale Sayers became the subject of the movie *Brian's Song*.

Tim Duncan

Duncan was the National Player of the Year in 1997. That same year, he repeated as the ACC's Player of the Year. He was named to the ACC first-team three times. He led Wake Forest to four straight twenty-win seasons and was the No. 1 pick in the 1997 NBA draft.

Chris Paul

Paul was the ACC Rookie of the Year in 2004 and a first-team All-ACC selection the following year. After his sophomore year, he entered the NBA draft and was the fourth player selected. He was the NBA's Rookie of the Year in 2006. He played on the USA's gold medal–winning teams in both the 2008 and 2012 Olympics.

Len Chappell

Chappell became Wake Forest's first consensus All-American in 1962. That year, he led Wake Forest to its first and only Final Four appearance. He was named the ACC Player of the Year in 1961 and 1962 and was a member of the All-ACC first-team three times. He remains the only player in ACC history to average more than thirty points (30.1) in a season.

ARENA

Lawrence Joel Veterans Memorial Coliseum: After playing its home games in the Greensboro Coliseum since the early 1980s, Wake Forest moved into the Lawrence Joel Veterans Memorial Coliseum for the 1989-90 season. The arena has a capacity of 14,665. The Demon Deacons' first game in Lawrence Joel was an exhibition game against Statiba of the Soviet Union on November 11, 1989.

STADIUM

BB&T Field: Wake Forest began playing in Groves Stadium in 1940 when the university was still located in its original location of Wake Forest, North Carolina. The 20,000-seat stadium was named in honor of Henry H. Groves Sr., whose gift to the university helped fund the original stadium.

The Demon Deacons played their games at Groves Stadium until 1955 when the university moved to Winston-Salem. Wake Forest played its games at Bowman Gray Stadium. Wake Forest opened up its own stadium in 1968 and called it Groves Stadium. The school re-named the football stadium BB&T Field prior to the 2007 season.

CUSE CONNECTION

ALL-TIME FOOTBALL RECORD VS. SYRACUSE: 1-1

Last meeting 2011: Syracuse 36, Wake Forest 29 (OT)

ALL-TIME BASKETBALL RECORD VS. SYRACUSE: 0-1

Last meeting 2001: Syracuse 74, Wake Forest 67 (Preseason NIT, New York City)

Len Chappell and the Nats: After finishing his college career at Wake Forest, Len Chappell was drafted by the NBA's Syracuse Nationals. He was the fourth player selected in the 1962 NBA draft. He spent the 1962-63 season in Syracuse. That year turned out to be the last season in Syracuse for the Nationals as the franchise moved to Philadelphia. Chappell averaged 8.9 points and 5.8 rebounds as a rookie for the Nats. His NBA career lasted nine years. He played in the 1964 NBA All-Star Game as a member of the New York Knicks and also spent one year in the ABA with the Dallas Chaparrals.

Jamesville-DeWitt High School: Wake Forest and Syracuse share a common bond thanks to a Class A public high school located just outside the Syracuse city limits. Wake Forest's Tyler Cavanaugh and Syracuse's Brandon Triche and Dajuan Coleman were all teammates at Jamesville-DeWitt. Coleman and Cavanaugh were classmates, graduating in 2012. Cavanaugh and Coleman helped the Red Rams to three New York State Class A state title games, two championships and one semifinal appearance.

Demon Deacon–Orange links: Syracuse coach Jim Boeheim and Wake Forest star Chris Paul were both part of the U.S. Olympic basketball team in 2008 and 2012. Boeheim was an assistant coach, and Paul played on both teams.... In the first meeting between the two schools' football teams, Wake Forest won the 2006 season-opener 20-10 over Syracuse. Wake finished that year in the FedEx Orange Bowl.... Syracuse and Wake Forest have played just once on the basketball court, but the two teams nearly met in the 2003 NCAA Tournament. Wake Forest was the No. 2 seed in the East bracket, but the Demon Deacons were upset in the second round by Auburn, which then lost to No. 3 seed Syracuse in the Sweet 16. Syracuse went onto win the national championship.

MASCOT

Wake Forest's sports teams were originally called the Fighting Baptists, owing to the school's early connection to the Baptist Convention. In 1923, a newspaper reporter covering the Wake Forest football team's win against Duke described the team as having "fought like Demons." The phrase eventually resulted in the term "Demon Deacons."

In 1941, a student named Jack R. Baldwin, acting on a fraternity brother's dare, dressed up as an old-time Baptist deacon with top hat, tuxedo, and dark umbrella. The nattily-attired Deacon would become the school's mascot. The current mascot with its oversized Deacon's head debuted in 1980.

FIGHT SONG

"O Here's to Wake Forest"

O here's to Wake Forest

A glass of the finest

Red ruddy, Rhenish filled up to the brim

Her sons they are many

Unrivaled by any

With hearts o'erflowing, we will sing a hymn

(Chorus)

Rah, Rah, Wake Forest, Rah

Old Alma Mater's sons are we

We'll herald the story and die for her glory

Old Gold and Black is ever waving high.

OTHER SPORTS

The Wake Forest men's golf team has won three NCAA titles and finished in the top ten on twenty-three other occasions. The Demon Deacons were NCAA champions in 1974, 1975, and 1986. In 1974, Curtis Strange, who would later win back-to-back U.S. Opens, eagled the 18th hole to give Wake Forest its first national title while also securing medalist honors. In 1975, Wake won again only this time Jay Haas earned medalist honors. Some of the other notable alumni of Wake's golf program include Arnold Palmer, Lanny Wadkins, Billy Andrade, Bill Haas, and Gary Hallberg.

GAME DAY

MEDIA

Broadcasting the Game: WBRF-FM 98.1 in Triad

Covering the Demon Deacons: www.journalnow.com (*Winston-Salem Journal*), www.news-record.com (*Greensboro News & Record*)

TAILGATING

The best places to tailgate are the open parking lots at the LJVM Coliseum. Buses, RVs, rental trucks, and trailers will be directed to the LJVM Coliseum lots as these types of vehicles are not permitted in the BB&T Field lots. General Public Parking in the LJVM lots is $8. For questions on parking at LJVM Coliseum, call 336-725-5635.

If you don't have a tailgate set-up, fans can go to Deacon Tailgate Town on Baity Street right across from the Deacon Tower. It's a family-friendly atmosphere with games, food, and music. About two hours before kickoff, the Wake Forest band, cheerleaders, and the Demon Deacon arrive at the Deacon Tailgate Town as the Wake Forest players arrive for the Deacon Walk.

SHUTTLE

With plenty of parking space availability near BB&T Field and the Lawrence Joel Veterans Memorial Coliseum, fans really have no need for a shuttle. However, golf cart shuttles are available to assist disabled, injured, or elderly fans. Fans may request a cart from a parking lot attendant or by calling 336-758-4263. Volunteers are available at Gates 1, 2, 3, and 5 to help fans to their seats.

TRADITIONS

Rolling the Quad: Wake Forest students celebrate the Demon Deacons' biggest athletic victories by covering Hearns Plaza in toilet paper or "rolling the quad." The practice began in the early 1960s after the university had moved to its current location in 1956. It's believed that Wake Forest students got the idea from students at nearby R.J. Reynolds High School who papered the trees on their campus after major sporting wins.

Opening of the Gate: It's not exactly steeped in history, but the Wake Forest tradition of Opening the Gate is a pretty cool one. In 2008, Wake Forest officials came up with a new idea for Demon Deacons' home football games. For each game at BB&T Field, the university brings back an honored guest who opens the gate and leads the team onto the field.

ABOUT TOWN

Winston-Salem was founded in 1753 as a settlement for the Moravian Church known as Bethabara. When the settlers decided on a primary site for their settlement, they named it Salem. Many of the original buildings in the settlement have been restored and are now part of the Old Salem Museum & Gardens. In 1852, the residents of Salem sold some land to Forsyth County, upon which a county seat was founded. The town was named Winston in honor of Joseph Winston, who was a Revolutionary War hero. The two towns were officially incorporated as Winston-Salem in 1913.

In 1875, Richard Joshua Reynolds built his first tobacco factory in Winston. The R.J. Reynolds Tobacco Company has played a huge role in Winston-Salem's development over the years. The Wachovia National Bank

was founded here in 1879. In 1901, J. Wesley Hanes began making men's socks at his Shamrock Hosiery Mills. His company is known today as Hanesbrands, the maker of men's underwear. And in 1937 the first Krispy Kreme donut shop opened in Winston-Salem.

Today, Winston-Salem is called the "Twin City" for obvious reasons and "City of the Arts and Innovation" for its thriving arts community and technological research facilities.

LODGING

Graylyn: The Graylyn Conference Center isn't a hotel, it's an estate. It's located just minutes from downtown Winston-Salem on a fifty-five-acre property. The Graylyn dates back to 1874 as the home of Bowman Gray Sr. Its stone façade invokes that of a British estate. *1900 Reynolda Rd., Winston-Salem, NC 27106, 800-472-9596, www.graylyn.com*

Courtyard by Marriott: The Courtyard by Marriott is located within a mile of the Wake Forest campus. It's within walking distance of both the Lawrence Joel Veterans Memorial Coliseum and BB&T Field. *3111 University Parkway, Winston-Salem, NC 27105, 336-727-1277, www.marriott.com*

Twin City Quarter: The quarter is located in the heart of Winston-Salem. It offers a wide variety of shops, restaurants, and bars. The hub is the Benton Convention Center and the area is served by two upscale hotels—a full-service Marriott and an Embassy Suites. The Winston-Salem Marriott's number is 336-725-3500 and the Embassy Suites is 336-724-7300.

EATING

Village Tavern: The Village Tavern has multiple locations around the country, including the restaurant in the historic Reynolda Village in Winston-Salem. The Village Tavern is known for putting its own twist on traditional American fare. The menu offers everything from steaks to pizza, and the desserts are homemade. *221 Reynolda Village, Winston-Salem, NC 27106, 336-748-0221, www.villagetavern.com*

Putters Patio & Grill: Putters has been around since 1955 and has long been a favorite of Wake Forest fans. It's located near the Lawrence Joel Veterans Memorial Coliseum, so it's perfect for the pre- or post-game meal. Steaks, subs, and sandwiches are served in a comfortable atmosphere that includes flat-screen TVs and an inviting patio. *3005 Bonhurst Dr., Winston-Salem, NC 27106, 336-724-9990, www.putterspatioandgrill.com*

Little Richards BBQ: Little Richards opened in 1991 with owner Richard Berrier serving up hickory-smoked barbeque with his own secret sauce. Simply put: It's heaven in your mouth. It's so good that there's now a second location in Winston-Salem, but we're using the address for the original. *4885 Country Club Rd., Winston-Salem, NC 27106, 336-760-3457, www.eatmopig.com*

SIGHTSEEING

Old Salem: The Old Salem Museum and Gardens offers a truly unique experience. Or three. There's the Town of Salem, which allows visitors to experience the historic settlement of Salem. There's the Gardens at Old Salem. And there's the Museum of Early Southern Decorative Arts, or MESDA, which boasts a range of Southern artistry and crafts.

Wait Chapel: Wait Chapel, which opened in 1956, is named after Samuel Wait (1789-1867), who was a leading Baptist minister in North Carolina. The Chapel is the largest non-athletic indoor setting on the Reynolda Campus with a seating capacity of 2,250. It houses the Williams Organ, which has over 4,600 pipes, and the Harris Carillon, which consists of forty-eight cast bronze bells. *1834 Wake Forest Rd., Winston-Salem, NC 27106, 336-758-5210, chaplain.studentlife.wfu.edu/weddings-events/wait-chapel/*

Bethabara Park: Settled in 1753, Historic Bethabara Park, a National Historic Landmark, is the site of the first Moravian settlement in the Carolinas. *2147 Bethabara Rd., Winston-Salem, NC 27106, 336-924-8191, www.bethabarapark.org*

SHOPPING

Reynolda Village: Reynolda Village includes many unique shops and restaurants. It's located minutes from the Wake Forest campus. *2201 Reynolda Rd., Winston-Salem, NC 27106, www.reynoldavillage.com*

Piedmont Craftsmen: The gallery is located in the heart of Winston-Salem's Downtown Arts District. It includes the works of more than three hundred artists and is worth a visit whether you're looking or buying. *601 North Trade St., Winston-Salem, NC 27101, 336-725-1516, www.piedmontcraftsmen.org*

NIGHTLIFE

Finnigan's Wake: Finnigan's Wake is more than just an Irish bar, although it's a really good Irish bar. The full name is Finnigan's Wake Irish Pub and Kitchen, and don't discount the kitchen. Finnigan's offers a family-friendly restaurant plus a pub with forty beers on tap and a wide selection of whiskeys. *620 Trade St., Winston-Salem, NC 27101, 336-723-0322, www.finniganswake.net*

First Street Draught House: The First Street Draught House is located on the edge of downtown Winston-Salem. It's both restaurant and bar with a large patio. The beer selection includes several North Carolina brews, including the Olde Hickory Table Rock Pale. Cheers! *1500 West First St., Winston-Salem, NC 27104, 336-722-6950, www.firststreetdraughthouse.com*

LAST-MINUTE TIPS

Where to Shop: Hanes Mall is located just off I-40 at the junction of I-421. There are big block stores and smaller shops. There's also a Deacon Shop where you can find all your Wake Forest gear. *3320 Silas Creek Parkway, Winston-Salem, NC 27103, 336-765-8321, www. shophanesmall.com*

Where to Buy Tickets: The best place to find Wake Forest tickets is at *www.wakeforestsports.com.*

Foothills Brewing: Foothills Brewing takes brewing hand-crafted beers on site to a completely different place—the kitchen. Foothills incorporates its beers into its recipes, including an ale-based ketchup. Some of the beers on tap include Carolina Blonde, Salem Gold, and Sexual Chocolate. *638 W. Fourth St., Winston-Salem, NC 27104, 336-722-6950, www.foothillsbrewing.com*

TRAVELING TO WINSTON-SALEM?

The Piedmont Triad International Airport serves the Winston-Salem, Greensboro, High Point area. It's located in Greensboro and is about twenty minutes from the Wake Forest campus. Winston-Salem is ninety minutes from Charlotte and two hours from Raleigh. It takes about eleven hours to drive from Syracuse to Wake Forest.